School Violence...
Calming the Storm

A guide to creating a fight-free school environment

School Violence... Calming the Storm

A guide to creating a fight-free school environment

Dr. Margaret R. Dolan
Foreword by Mychal Wynn

Comments from schools that have started the Fight-Free Process:

On Principal's Day, the students submitted letters expressing how much they appreciated a Fight-Free school and all of the incentives. Our fights were reduced by 50%. We observed a student awareness of the problem of fighting. Team efforts encouraged the teachers to work more closely to ensure that their students would not fight on the playground. A sense of school spirit was also created as students cheered our Fight-Free Song and worked toward the rewards of remaining fight free. Parents saw the Fight-Free process as a positive way to improve student attitudes and to help ensure a safer playground for their children. Several parents checked in with me periodically to see how we were doing each month.

> Frank Thouvenot, Principal
> Bridgeway Elementary School
> Bridgeton, MO

The Fight-Free process shows more community spirit. It is a common language spoken by students, staff, and bus drivers. Kids have more ownership of their behavior, and parents use Fight Free at home. We developed a Steering Committee composed of administrators, teachers, parents, and students. We developed, implemented, and monitored the process. Also, it was tied to the already-existing Conflict Mediation Program.

> Michael Ceruttie, Principal
> Wren Hollow Elementary School
> Ballwin, MO

Fighting has been reduced by 60% since Fight Free began. The Fight-Free process has had a positive effect. The number of fighting incidents has been reduced and more positive ways of dealing with conflict has resulted. It gives a very visible focus to the students to think before they act.

> Dr. Robert Cowles, Principal
> Duchesne Elementary School
> Florissant, MO

Implementing Fight-Free has changed the culture in terms of what is cool; it is cool to be fight free. The Fight-Free process has carried over to actions outside of school — going to and coming from school — fewer fights and positive peer pressure.

> Linda Rowold, Principal
> Parmer Lane Elementary School
> Austin, TX

In our school, we noticed the students used peer pressure to keep the Fight-Free Banner up. "Don't cause a fight; we don't want the Fight-Free Banner to come down." Students will keep other students from fighting. Fights were reduced by 50% since implementing Fight Free.

Susan Whiting, Principal
Kellison Elementary School
Fenton, MO

A strength of the Fight-Free process for us is that we are giving attention to the fight-free students rather than to the fighting students. Heroes at our school are the students who do not fight back.

Rob Sainz, Principal
Carmen Trails Elementary School
Manchester, MO

The Fight-Free Schools process has made a difference in our climate because the students help to regulate students from fighting and use peer pressure in a positive way. In planning our Fight-Free incentive, we planned a co-curricular activity. Fight-Free students get to choose their desired activity at the end of each quarter.

Jack Williams, Principal
Hoech Middle School
St. Ann, MO

We named our Fight-Free program "Peace Makers." If there was no Fight Free in place, the rate of violence would severely increase. The program is positive, it is in front of the students constantly. We have Peace Maker school forms and reports about catching students being good. I'm sold on it. You must keep it dynamic and changing to make it work.

Frank Wojeck, Principal
Union School School
East St. Louis, MO

Dr. Peggy Dolan is a principal of "America's Best Practice" Award-Winning school and the first Fight-Free School, McNair Elementary in Hazelwood, Missouri.

To schedule parent training, staff development, or keynote presentations contact:

Rising Sun Publishing/Training and Staff Development

(800) 524-2813
e-mail: speaking@rspublishing.com

FIRST EDITION 1998

School Violence...Calming The Storm
ISBN 1-880463-14-8
Copyright © 1998 by Margaret R. Dolan, Ph.D.
Copyright © 1998 Rising Sun Publishing, Inc.

All rights reserved. Classroom teachers may reproduce limited quantities of the activities for use in their individual classrooms. Copying for entire schools, and/or school districts, or use in curriculum programs is prohibited without the expressed written permission from Rising Sun Publishing, Inc. Video and audio tapes, charts, posters, and other support materials are available from Rising Sun Publishing, Inc.

No part of this book may be reproduced or transmitted in any form or by any means, electronic or mechanical, including photocopying, recording, or storing in any information storage and retrieval system for commercial purposes.

P.O. Box 70906
Marietta, Georgia 30007-0906
(800) 524-2813
e-mail: info@rspublishing.com
web site: http://www.rspublishing.com

Printed in the United States of America.

Dedication

With fond memories of my childhood supper table, where the seeds of this book were planted, I dedicate this book to my brothers: Ed, Tim, and Dennis, and in loving memory of our mom, Della Rose Dolan, and our dad, Edward Francis Dolan.
I thank them for the supper time "table talk."

Acknowledgments

I gratefully acknowledge the following who assisted in creating this manual and who share the Fight-Free Mission with me:

My niece, Jennifer Christy Dolan, who created the title of the book.

My niece, Molly Ann Dolan, who wrote the postscript.

My mentor, Dr. William Rebore, for writing the Preface.

My secretary, Jo Lynn Ward, who assisted and supported me.

The McNair students, staff, and parents for being the first Fight-Free School in the U.S.A.

County Executive, Buzz Westfall, for his sponsorship and continued support.

Congressman Richard Gephardt and his Washington office representative, Cathy Dente, for their support.

Jeff Shackelford, photographer for Lifetouch Studios.

Our Editor, Denise Mitchell Smith, for ensuring the clarity of our message.

Mychal Wynn for his belief in the Fight-Free Mission.

All Fight-Free Schools who fly their flags proudly.

In memory

To the students and teachers who have lost their lives as a result of school violence.
In your memory we are dedicated to helping all schools to become safe places.

TABLE OF CONTENTS

From the Publisher	IX
Foreword	X
About the Author	XII
Preface	XIII

1. **Philosophy and Background of Fight Free** 1
2. **The Pilot Program** 10
   - Instructional Activity 12
3. **The Fight-Free School Mission** 17
   - The Fight-Free Campaign 18
   - The Teachers 18
   - Planning with Teachers 19
   - Behavior Workshop 20
   - Defining a Fight 22
   - Thinking Fight Free 22
   - Acting as a Fight-Free Role Model 23
   - Parents 25
4. **Launching the Fight-Free Program** 27
5. **Government** 32
6. **Law Enforcement** 36
   - Community and Business Participation 37
7. **Most Often-Asked Questions about the Fight-Free Schools Program** 39
8. **Fight Free Goes Preschool** 46
9. **Carmen Trails Elementary School Implementation Strategy** 49

   Appendix
   - Fight-Free Activities Overview 58
   - Section I: Planning 60
   - Section II: Behavior Workshop 63
   - Section III: KHFAAOOTY Bear Activities 73
   - Section IV: Classroom Activities 85
   - Section V: Multiple Intelligences Activities 102
   - Section VI: Additional Resources 121

School Violence...Calming the Storm

FROM THE PUBLISHER

My first introduction to Peggy Dolan came by means of a telephone call one day from Peggy. "Hello Mychal? A good friend of mine, Dee Blassie, suggested that I call you. I am looking for a publisher and she thinks that you are a wonderful person and I want to work with you!" Peggy went on to tell me about her Fight-Free Process and about how it had virtually eliminated violence at her school. As she described her process, I could immediately see that it was a process that all educators could use, parents could appreciate, and one that children could excel in.

I told Peggy that I thought her approach to fostering a positive school culture and climate was an integral component of a process that we here at Rising Sun Publishing use for training schools in "The Change Continuum." We believe that children should come to school with passion and purpose in pursuit of their dreams and aspirations. Naturally, in helping students to discover and pursue their dreams and aspirations we must make the school and classroom a safe and risk-free learning environment; a place where children can try and fail without fear of put-downs or ridicule from their classmates; a place where children are free from the threat of verbal or physical abuse. Anyone who believes that words can't hurt is tragically out of touch with what goes on in America's schools. Far too many children dread going to school because of the fear of being put down, picked on, or otherwise singled out for being different.

Peggy's Fight-Free process represents one of the key components in turning schools and classrooms into places of passion and purpose–places where our children are free to explore, experiment, make mistakes, and learn. While we have taken God out of schools, Peggy's genius has brought divine inspiration back into the minds and hearts of teachers, students, and their parents.

I am glad that Peggy made that phone call and we are honored to be a part of the process of sharing Fight-Free Schools with anyone interested in the emotional well-being, physical safety, and in providing a safe and nurturing academic environment for children everywhere.

Dr. Margaret R. Dolan

FOREWORD

I have had the opportunity to work with K-12 schools throughout the U.S. for the past sixteen years. Over that period of time, I have come to identify a number of components in what I term, "The Change Continuum," the process of change common to every school. Each school exists along this continuum. Each school deals with the issues of change unique to its school community, defining and working toward goals, and eradicating issues or obstacles that hinder it from achieving its vision. That vision may include higher academic achievement, higher test scores, fewer discipline problems, increased student attendance, lower teacher turnover, or any of a multitude of other short–and long-term goals determined by the stakeholders of its school community.

While researchers develop data and publishers market programs, few would deny that many schools are doing little to educate and protect the children entrusted to the school each day of the school year. Oddly enough, while the many stakeholders in school communities argue, debate, discuss, demand, and demean each other, the most significant stakeholders, the children, have no advocate, no voice, little choice, and are rarely if ever a part of the solution to the very issues that threaten their lives and their learning. The more I listen to the arguments, watch the failed programs, and witness the hundreds of thousands of America's school-aged children being victimized by an institution that views them only as test score subjects and numbers for increasing federal dollars and local tax assessments, I am committed to becoming their advocate. This is why I have chosen to work with Peggy Dolan. While others would explain away the violence in America's schools as: the breakdown of the two-parent family; socioeconomic levels of students; ineffective classroom management by teachers; the massive exposure of children to violence through print, video, and music media; the proliferation of drugs and gangs; or to the violent pop culture role models, Dr. Dolan has taken the position, "I cannot change the many ills of America today, but I can foster a culture in my school that violence is an unacceptable method for resolving conflicts."

While others debate, Dr. Dolan strategizes; while others discuss, Dr. Dolan implements; while others spread blame, Dr. Dolan accepts responsibility. I don't believe in "Programs." If Peggy would have called me and said that she had a "Program" that could reduce violence, I would have given her my blessings. But I would not have given her my time. Fight Free is not a program but a process. A process of changing the way that the stakeholders in a school community help children to make healthy choices. This is real learning, not the abstract kind that is common to "Programs." Real learning is wholistic, engaging, and eternal. It introduces an individual to new knowledge; helps the individual to apply that knowledge in meaningful, real-life applications; helps the individual to internalize the knowledge acquired; and, helps the individual to evolve to higher levels of knowledge, in essence, a higher consciousness.

More metal detectors, more police, video cameras, harsher discipline methods, zero tolerance policies, or, as one insane lawmaker suggested, "Let's give teachers guns," will not guarantee the safety of our children. They are only reactionary measures needed because of a systemic, institutionalized unwillingness to engage our children in meaningful, relevant, discussion, debate, and analysis of the critical life issues that they are confronted with each day in our schools and classrooms. Such approaches are not designed to increase consciousness, but to control our children as we camouflage our failings. Peggy, on the other hand, just goes about the business of educating children, teaching them how to make positive choices, and fostering an environment conducive to learning, growing, and having fun.

I have chosen to publish this book because I know that the thinkers and doers who design methods that work have little time or inclination to play the politics that get "Programs" adopted in schools. They are too busy doing, demonstrating, and contributing to the emotional and intellectual development of our children. I am, however, firmly convinced that they will be remembered by our children long after those content with arguing, debating, and discussing how to control our children. Peggy Dolan is a pioneer of the present, a vanguard of the future, and an advocate for our children. She has already ensured her place in the lasting memories of hundreds of children and their parents. The Fight-Free Process works when a school community is diligent and determined to work through it without metal detectors, police, the threat of zero tolerance, or arming teachers. It simply works because it is a wholistic approach, implemented through clear and cohesive instructional strategies, and respects children as divinely intelligent beings capable of achieving higher consciousness and making healthy choices.

We are limited only by the scope of our vision. We are bound only by the magnitude of our dreams.
– Mychal Wynn

Dr. Margaret R. Dolan

ABOUT THE AUTHOR

January 27, 1998

Dear Dr. Dolan:

I want to thank you for the fight-free environment here at McNair. Having taught in a district where fights occurred almost on a daily basis, I had no idea that a fight-free school, such as McNair, existed. There are so many things, in addition to teaching academics, that a teacher must deal with on a daily basis. I am so thankful that my safety and/or the safety of my students is not one of them.

I often hear stories from my students about other schools they've attended and how they were afraid because "There were fights all the time," and if they told they'd "get beat up, too." When I tell them that they should feel safe no matter what school they attend the response I get is, "I didn't know there was a school where there was no fighting." So, Peggy, you and your "Fight-Free Program" have definitely made a difference! Thank you, and keep up the good work.

Sincerely,

Linda Kain
Special Education Teacher
Behavior Disordered and Learning Disabled

This letter, more than anything else, tells who Peggy Dolan is and what she has meant to our children. Having served in the field of education for twenty-eight years, Peggy has been a classroom teacher; a teacher of the Gifted and Talented; a curriculum writer; a publisher of children's stories; and a guest on numerous television and radio programs with her vision of hope. Recognized as an Outstanding Young Woman of the Year, Outstanding Teacher of the Year, and Who's Who in Educational Administration, she has served on the Governor's Task Force on Violence in School and as a panelist on the Summit on Crime. She has been an extraordinary educator and child advocate throughout her distinguished career. She has conceptualized and pioneered a revolutionary and visionary Fight-Free process.

Dr. Dolan is presently the principal of McNair Elementary School in Hazelwood, Missouri.

PREFACE

Violence in schools: Will it become the legacy of the Twentieth Century or is it simply a reflection of the society that we have created? It seems as if little time elapses between headlines and/or new reports about a shooting at a school. Even more surprising, these acts are occurring not necessarily in large urban high schools that have been historically identified with violence, but in elementary and middle schools located in suburban and rural communities. In Arkansas, two boys, ages 11 and 13, kill four classmates and a teacher; in Missouri, a young high school student is killed between classes. Unfortunately, reactions to these intermittent acts have resulted in calls for metal detectors, video surveillance, locked doors, and an almost prison mentality among education's harshest critics.

While these horrendous acts grab the headlines, there are many episodes of violence in schools every day. Neighborhood disagreements, immature behavior, or misunderstandings often escalate into fights among classmates daily. Together with the occasional acts of severe violence, these instances have now risen to the point that safety and security issues are the number one concern of parents as they send their children off to school.

The reality of violence in our schools places in context the importance of Dr. Peggy Dolan's ***Fight-Free Schools***. Her success, first at McNair Elementary School, and later at schools throughout the area, is built on the positive reinforcement of student behavior. Fight-Free Schools has been introduced in numerous elementary and middle schools with a minimum of cost and tremendous success. This success has attracted the attention of local, state, and national leaders as they work on legislation to stem the violence in our schools.

Principals and teachers in private, parochial, and public schools owe it to themselves to consider Dr. Dolan's *Fight-Free Schools*. It could very well be the first step toward creating a truly safe and secure environment for the children of our communities, and just may impact and reverse the tide of societal violence.

William T. Rebore, Ph.D.
Saint Louis University
May, 1998

Dr. Margaret R. Dolan

I had no control over where my students came from. I had no control over the values communicated in their respective households. I had no control over the negative aggressive images that they were exposed to each day through the television and music played in their households. However, I could control the process by which we would introduce instructional strategies and reinforce desired behavior each day in our school. No child would be a victim in our school. Each child would have the opportunity to succeed. Each child would have the opportunity to pursue their dreams and aspirations without fear of ridicule, put-downs, or the threat of physical violence.

– Dr. Peggy Dolan
Principal, McNair Elementary

CHAPTER 1

Philosophy and Background of Fight Free

Congratulations McNair students, we have 520 fight free students in our school today. The fight-free flag is flying to proclaim that we have 520 students who observed our rule: KEEP HANDS, FEET, AND ALL OTHER OBJECTS TO YOURSELF.

– Dr. Peggy Dolan, Principal
First Fight-Free School in the USA

Little did I know as a beginning principal that the accolade you have just read would serve as the key instructional tool I would use on a daily basis to promote a positive school climate and culture, in essence a fight-free school. After fostering a positive school climate and culture via the instructional activities, positive daily reinforcement through audible and visual signals, our school community was able to provide a safe, risk-free learning environment for our students.

Among the first indicators of a positive school climate was the language that students and teachers were using with each other. Teachers began to lead the cheering section when the daily announcements were indicative of total school participation in fight-free behavior. "Way to go, class. Let's be a part of that number tomorrow!" School assemblies began with students, in unison, reciting the number one school rule: "Keep Hands, Feet, and All Other Objects to Yourself." Students were overheard reminding each other of fight-free behavior, "Hey, let's not fight. We don't want to cause the flag to come down." On the playground, when a dispute over a "safe" or "out" in kickball occurred, Write-Not-Fight forms were used to help mediate hurt feelings during any verbal confrontations. The positive school climate that enhanced the learning environment at McNair was reflected in overall higher standardized test scores and the need for fewer student retentions. These gains were achieved despite a decline in the socioeconomic level of the school community, evidenced by the increased percentage of students receiving free and reduced breakfast and lunch. I had no control over where my students came from. I had no control over the values communicated in their respective households. I had no control over the negative aggressive images that they were exposed to each day through the television and music played in their households. However, I could control the process by which we would introduce instructional strategies and reinforce desired behavior each day in our school. No child would be a victim in our school. Each child would have the opportunity to succeed. Each child would have the opportunity to pursue their dreams and aspirations without fear of ridicule, put-downs, or the threat of physical violence.

Dr. Margaret R. Dolan

My goals as a beginning principal were to be the instructional leader of the school and to maintain the positive school climate that effective schools' research mandated. However, as the principal, I soon learned that there would be obstacles which I would have to overcome in creating a positive school climate and in serving as a role model for instruction.

The obstacles of every principal are: recess, cafeteria, restroom breaks, hallways (including stairwells), and school buses. Don't forget that the principal is in charge of student behavior on the way to school and on the way home from school. My studies for a doctorate in administration did not prepare me for the times between 11:00 A.M. and 1:00 P.M.

At both national and local Fight-Free Seminars, I am greeted by head nodding and groans in unanimous agreement. The definitive course offering on how to interact with teachers, students, and parents, and in partnership with the community on the issue of school violence has yet to be written. The common language that puts all of the contingencies that principals face on the same page, in my mind, was yet to be articulated. As a principal, even when no one else did, my task was to keep the peace.

Instead of instructional leader, I won the starring role as Judge Judy. In my role, I judiciously investigated the origins of hits, kicks, shoves, pushes, walk-by elbows, bites, name-calling, face-making, and inappropriate gesturing, not to mention inappropriate language (verbal, written, or graphic). After a thorough investigation, the inquisition process was supposed to lead me to a fair verdict. Instead, it led me in circles with such depositions as:

"She started it."

"No, she started it."

"No, we weren't fighting we were just pushing."

"No, we weren't fighting we were playing around."

"He hit me, so I hit him back."

"My dad said when anyone hits me at school, I have his permission to hit back, and if you don't like it you can call him yourself."

"No, it wasn't a fight we just accidentally hit each other while tumbling down the stairs."

"No, I didn't really tear the sink out of the wall in the restroom. We were all reaching for the faucet, and I just got pushed harder than the rest."

Since its beginning, the Fight-Free Program has been a powerful influence at Carman Trails Elementary. Children have replaced hitting with a more mature response to resolving conflicts. Office referrals for discipline have diminished; attention is toward learning. Parents respond to our discipline without defensiveness. They simply say, "We know what you are trying to do at Carman Trails Elementary."

Fight Free has been an important, positive change to our culture.

**Robert Sainz
Principal**

School Violence...Calming the Storm

"No, I didn't hit anyone, I was just throwing rocks." (A certified teacher was the eye witness.) The next phase of the process leads me to call the parents to inform them of the problem and consequences administered (Judge Judy would call it, "My verdict!"). The parental responses varied, however, here are a few:

"Well, if my son hit someone, then he was provoked. I told my son if he is hit, to hit back, no matter what anyone at school says."

"Well, Dr. Dolan, you don't understand boys. Boys will be boys and I'm happy to know my son isn't a sissy."

"If my daughter said she didn't do it, then she didn't do it. She has never lied. Are you calling my daughter a liar?"

"What punishment are you giving the other student?"

"How do you know it was my son's rock that hit the window?"

"My daughter will not serve detention for defending herself."

"You go ahead and take care of my son and do whatever you want when he is there. You have my permission to hit him. Give him a good old-fashioned spanking and that will teach him."

By this time, it is four o'clock. School has been dismissed, I cannot reach some of the parents, and I will have to follow up the next morning. I am just hoping to complete this round before 11:00 A.M. the next day since the entire cycle will start all over again.

Something is wrong with this picture. Now add the results of the school's Annual Report to an already dreary state of affairs, and the data is clear: **520 students, 55 fights, 27 suspensions for fighting,** and yet I am told that I have a "good" school. McNair is one of the last of the Beaver Cleaver schools: sidewalks, a long list of parent volunteers, and 100% PTA membership. As I analyzed the report, I noticed that detentions were at an all-time high. Detention is one hour before school begins. A staff member is paid via an extra-duty contract to function as the detention supervisor. The solution to my problem was certainly not more detentions. My detention supervisor was able to purchase a mink coat with her detention earnings! Was this report evidence that I had attained my goal of being an effective instructional leader and was the overall school climate safe and orderly, not to mention positive?

> A report conducted by the National School Boards Association concluded that violence had reached "epidemic proportions." Three-fourth of the school districts polled in the study (729 school districts) stated that their districts had experienced an increase in violence during the past five years; not only in urban areas, but in suburban and rural areas as well.

Dr. Margaret R. Dolan

Could the disorder I was feeling in my school have something to do with the school violence issue that was surfacing nationwide? Reports in published readings were coming across my desk with statistics showing that fighting in schools in the last five years was increasing. A report conducted by the National School Boards Association concluded that violence had reached "epidemic proportions." Three-fourth of the school districts polled in the study (729 school districts) stated that their districts had experienced an increase in violence during the past five years; not only in urban areas, but in suburban and rural areas as well.

In a 1993 survey conducted by the magazine, <u>Executive Educator</u>, in conjunction with a research team from Xavier University in Cincinnati, Ohio, the trend of violent acts was traced as commonplace in high school students. Now more acts of violence are infiltrating middle and elementary schools. Conclusions drawn on the elementary level are that girls' fighting is up 45% and boys' fighting is up 43%. Studying the drug increase in the elementary environment, I noted a 22% increase which was significantly lower than the fighting statistic. However, in my dilemmas faced while being Judge Judy from 11:00 A.M. to 1:00 P.M., I was never confronted with a drug problem in my school.

Studying the statistics, I noticed that drugs were decreasing. However, I never had a drug problem in my school. I also never had a gun or a shooting or a knifing in my school as reports showed other schools were experiencing. What was the drug education program offering that I was not? The fights were termed "kids' stuff." Did I really have to tolerate that? Did the students really have to tolerate being hit by other students even if I did not have a problem with guns or knives in the school? Why is there such an increase in violence in schools?

My reflections led me to think about expectations that teachers had of students when I started as a teacher some twenty-five years ago. The teachers taught the reading, writing, and arithmetic and the moms and dads took care of teaching how to behave. Even as a student, myself, some forty years ago, if the teacher called home to report a problem at school, then there was a problem at home until the problem at school was resolved. Societal expectations were that teachers taught reading, writing, and arithmetic in school and did not have time for teaching behavior. After all, mom and dad would handle that. If there were problems in the neighborhood, it stopped at the school house gate, because school was the safe harbor from the realities of domestic problems and violence in the streets. However, the realities of today's schools are before us in the headlines of newspapers that carry stories of students shooting students and teachers in schools in spite of metal detectors at the school house

> *When asked the question, "What is the least effective method of instruction?" teachers readily answer, "Lecture!"*
>
> *Yet when asked, "What is the most frequently utilized method of instruction for dealing with the negative behavior of children?" they moan, "Lecture."*
>
> *The negative behavior of children requires a commitment to instructional strategies. The lessons must be taught, the behaviors must be modeled, and the desired behaviors must be consistently reinforced.*
>
> **Mychal Wynn**
> *The Change Continuum*

gates. The headlines herald the fact that schools are not the safe harbors they were once thought to be. Something happened to the expectations that were alive and well forty years ago. Now the school is not the separate facility until we get to the real world. The school *is* the real world.

In some of today's schools over half of the class of twenty-five students are from single parent, foster care, or extended families. Not only does Beaver Cleaver not live here anymore, but Ward and/or June have flown the coop as well. Or, Ward and/or June are busy with careers. Day care, preschools, and latch keys have added an extra caretaker to the picture and the focus is not as clear as it used to be. So who is teaching the children behavioral expectations...everybody, anybody, nobody? The realities and expectations of schools have changed dramatically since I began teaching. We now serve breakfast and lunch; provide before school and after school care; provide counselors and social workers; provide transportation and health care; and provide character education. Can supper not be far behind?

The supper table is where Ed and Della Dolan held court every evening at 6:00 P.M., sharp. No matter where we were, we made sure the basketball was through the hoop, the last Camp Fire Girl song was sung, and we were present and accounted for at the Dolan table. That was where expectations for behavior were discussed with the Dolan clan. "The school called today and said you, Peggy, gave a disrespectful look to the teacher, and you, Eddie, decided to fight over a call on the playground." Or, "What did you do that was considerate today?" The seeds that we as children may have planted during the day were either weeded out or nurtured. The dialogue that took place seemed to serve as the bridge for us to form our own consciousness where appropriate behavior and interpersonal social skills were concerned.

Behavior expectations differ from parent to parent. No one wants their children hit. However, if their child gets hit, many parents give permission to hit back. Giving violence permission at the hitting level has somehow opened the door to the guns and the knives that we read about in today's headlines.

The evolution of violence has created a storm that is tearing through American communities. Nevertheless, as with most storm warnings, we do not want fear and panic to be our ultimate response. Looking at the total picture, I began to wonder how I could be an instructional leader who would educate students to solve problems in a peaceful manner now so that as citizens of the future, they could apply their lessons in interpersonal social skills as adults in society. The lessons learned at the supper table, in the classroom, or in the principal's office, as we work together

> *Behavior expectations differ from parent to parent. No one wants their children hit. However, if their child gets hit, many parents give permission to hit back. Giving violence permission at the hitting level has somehow opened the door to the guns and the knives that we read about in today's headlines. The evolution of violence has created a storm that is tearing through American communities. Nevertheless, as with most storm warnings, we do not want fear and panic to be our ultimate response. Looking at the total picture, I began to wonder how I could be an instructional leader who would educate students to solve problems in a peaceful manner now so that as citizens of the future, they could apply their lessons in interpersonal social skills as adults in society.*

Dr. Margaret R. Dolan

day-by-day, are the lessons of real life and what we will bring to our families and careers.

How would I make all of this possible as an instructional leader? Perhaps my Judge Judy techniques would be useful, after all, in helping me to investigate the big picture. Adding clues yielded the following:

The fights or single assaults were coming from the cafeteria, restroom, hallway, playground, on the bus, to and from school, and in all areas where there was no direct supervision or in areas where supervision consisted of managing large groups. I noticed that referrals for fights in the classroom were almost zero. Each classroom teacher designs and implements a clearly-communicated plan of discipline with rules and consequences posted. The classroom teacher is also supervising a smaller group of students.

> *In effective schools research, one of the leading indicators of a positive school climate is that the environment is safe and secure. Students feel safe in the school setting, safety and security being basic human needs. Didn't we all learn in our education psychology courses about Maslow's hierarchy of needs? One of the first needs to be tended as we grow is the need to feel safe and secure. Having this need satisfied leads us to the path for reaching self actualization as an adult.*

Clue 1: Under direct supervision, students were behaving appropriately perhaps storing their anger for one of the places in school where the teacher was not looking. Also, while individual teachers might achieve varying degrees of effectiveness in their individual classrooms the wide range of classroom management styles, individual expectations and consequences might unintentionally contribute to inconsistencies in the overall school climate. Therefore, a common language to articulate our common goals for all students in our school community would be needed. As the teacher must effectively manage the classroom, I, as principal, must effectively manage the school including the cafeteria, restrooms, hallways, playground, bus, and to and from school.

Clue 2: In our school, we had an excellent drug prevention education program whereby students joined a club to be drug free. There was a drug-free banner and we thought the program was so important that we devoted an entire week to celebrating being drug free. We even had a committee to design curriculum activities for drug education and the parents purchased ribbons for students and decorated the school. All of these efforts had been expended for drug prevention and yet I did not have students sent to my office for drugs. On a daily basis I had students sent to my office for fighting.

Clue 3: In effective schools research, one of the leading indicators of a positive school climate is that the environment is safe and secure. Students feel safe in the school setting, safety and security being basic human needs. Didn't we all learn in our education psychology courses about Maslow's hierarchy of

needs? One of the first needs to be tended as we grow is the need to feel safe and secure. Having this need satisfied leads us to the path for reaching self actualization as an adult.

Clue 4: Observing that the teachers in the classroom had a posted set of rules led me on a walk to the cafeteria. There, posted for all to see, were the cafeteria rules. In our student handbook were rules for bicycle safety, playground rules, and a code of conduct. We followed our district code of conduct guidelines. Certainly I was doing that with the number of detentions and suspensions I handed out.

Clue 5: Our district was now implementing video cameras on all buses to help monitor bus behavior. Did I need a video camera on the playground, in the hallway, etc.? What would that say to the students? "Be good because we are watching?" I read about schools that had installed metal detectors at the school door. What did this say to the hundreds of students passing through the detector each day? "We do not trust you. One of you may have a gun or a knife, so all will go through the metal detector." Seeing a metal detector at the front door may not ensure a safe environment. A student who shot another student in a local high school went through a metal detector and the school had increased security guards. Where, in all of these responses to the rise in violence, did we address the possibility that students could be intrinsically motivated?

> *I had never really taught the students expected behaviors. Parents say to the school, "You teach my kids how to behave. You have them all day." Teachers say, "Well, I should not have to teach students how to behave. I have to teach reading, math, and science and they should be learning behavior at home." Somewhere between home, latchkey, school, and the baby-sitter or day care, the job of teaching appropriate behavior was not being effectively taught, and continually reinforced on a consistent basis.*

Was I to be a participant in creating the safe environment? Extrinsic measures, although necessary, offer a "quick-fix" solution that is reactionary and would not yield the change in student behavior. I had never really taught the students expected behaviors. Parents say to the school, "You teach my kids how to behave. You have them all day." Teachers say, "Well, I should not have to teach students how to behave. I have to teach reading, math, and science and they should be learning behavior at home." Somewhere between home, latchkey, school, and the baby-sitter or day care, the job of teaching appropriate behavior was not being effectively taught, and continually reinforced on a consistent basis. We all expect appropriate behavior and we are disappointed when we do not get it. It is easy to point fingers and say, "It is not my problem." Teachers cannot teach because parents do not do their jobs. Parents rationalize that teachers see their children more in a day than parents. Principals find that it all lands in their lap.

Conclusion: Everybody is angry when students act inappropriately.

Gathering my clues and personal editorials, I thought that I would become the instructional

Dr. Margaret R. Dolan

> *What becomes name-calling and pushing in elementary school can become more violent as students grow bigger, stronger, and more aggressive. While we never question whether we will teach math, science, reading, writing, and social studies, we often don't consider teaching character values, conflict resolution, and appropriate social behavior in a democratic society until it becomes a problem.*

leader I had envisioned a good principal should be. My classroom would be the school and my lessons would teach children appropriate, interpersonal, social skills. These skills would not only be important to creating a positive school climate, but they would prove invaluable in achieving their long-term dreams and aspirations.

It did not take me long to learn that the least effective method of instruction was lecturing and to discover that the most frequently utilized method of instruction when dealing with children and their behaviors was, yes, you guessed it, "lecture!" I did not want the concepts of good citizenship and courteous and appropriate behavior to be abstract concepts to my students. I wanted them to know that contributing to our school as responsible citizens and embracing the qualities of courtesy and respect for others had immediate and long-term applications. These would become the very qualities embodied by those people who were living their dreams. These were the qualities of those who had reached the pinnacle of success in a multitude of careers from law to medicine, from teaching to preaching, from airline pilots to steam ship captains, from scientists to entrepreneurs.

By causing the students to become aware of the fight-free expectation, I would teach them how to behave in a variety of situations, and I would give them a system to use in our school setting for the inevitable confrontation. First and foremost, I realized that I would not lecture. Everything would come through instruction and dialogue with students. Inappropriate behavior cannot be lectured away; appropriate behavior is taught and reinforced. My goal was to assist students in realizing the value of appropriate behavior and their roles in being responsible for creating the environment. The result would be a Fight-Free School and a positive school climate which would enhance student academic achievement and provide greater opportunities for students to discover, pursue, and achieve their individual dreams and aspirations.

The reasons for eradicating verbal and physical violence from our schools is clear. As indicated in the "1998 White House Press Briefing on School Safety" the storm is threatening the very future of children:

So how safe are the schools? What can we tell you about the seriousness of crime in the schools? This study very clearly says that 100% of the serious violent crimes are in 10% of our schools. Some 90% of the 1,234 public schools surveyed had no incidents of serious violent crime in school year 1996-97...There were 424,000 incidents of all types of safety and crime problems in our schools, or about 10 incidents per 1,000 students. The most frequent category was physical attacks without a weapon, some 19,000 incidents.

School Violence...Calming the Storm

Pat Forgione, the National Commissioner for Education Statistics, stated that many less serious crimes, like fighting which didn't involve a weapon, would not have been reported to the police and, thus, would not have been reflected in the report,

> *"We were trying to get a sense of disruption to the institution and the school climate when you have to report to the police and it brings in that set of interaction. That meant it's very serious to us. So we were trying to avoid the trivial. And when you get to elementary especially, you can have a lot of interactions that have a range."*

Unfortunately, those of us in schools each day realize that what may be considered "trivial" today may become deadly tomorrow if effective intervention strategies are not in place (intervention, meaning instruction). What becomes name-calling and pushing in elementary school can become more violent as students grow bigger, stronger, and more aggressive. While we never question whether we will teach math, science, reading, writing, and social studies, we often don't consider teaching character values, conflict resolution, and appropriate social behavior in a democratic society until it becomes a problem. By then, some child has suffered long-lasting physical or emotional harm. Schools should not only become places of passion and purpose, but places where children are nurtured emotionally, enlightened academically, and are free from verbal abuse or physical attacks.

Adding wings to caterpillars does not create butterflies. A transformation is needed. Telling children not to fight and punishing them when they do does not create a fight-free consciousness. A transformation is needed.

— Ako Kambon
Executive Director,
Visionary Leaders Institute

Dr. Margaret R. Dolan

CHAPTER 2
The Pilot Program

Our children are not treated with sufficient respect as human beings, and yet from the moment they are born they have this right to respect. We keep children for too long, their world separate from the real world of life.
— Pearl S. Buck

Beginning the program, I had a perfect opportunity to model for staff and students the reporting system we would use, thanks to my custodian. He was very upset about a problem in the restroom. It seems that the boy's restroom on the second floor had a drainage problem every afternoon. Instead of using the hand towels to dry hands, they were being used to stop up the toilet. The frustrated custodian came to me around three o'clock and announced that the toilet on the second floor was stopped up again, that he was getting tired of it, and what was I going to do about it. I took the microphone to our public address system and made the following announcement: "Congratulations, boys and girls. We have 520 students in our school and there are 519 of you who know how to use the hand towels properly in the restroom. Tomorrow when I check on the restrooms, I'll bet that I will be able to announce that there are 520 students who know how to use hand towels properly." After school, a sixth grade teacher reported that one sixth grade boy sunk in his chair with a worried look on his face. The next day at three o'clock, I made the following announcement: "Congratulations, students of McNair. We have 520 students who know how to use the restroom appropriately. Thank you for helping to keep our restrooms in tip-top condition. I am proud of you. Keep up the outstanding effort."

Now that the students knew how I was going to behave, I began to teach them how I expected them to behave. I began to report, after recesses, how many students DID NOT fight. Each day we cheered as the number not fighting equaled the enrollment. When fighting was reduced, isolated hits, kicks, shoves or pushes continued. But now, students were not hitting back. I would be swift to administer consequences from the code of conduct to the individuals who had used physical aggression. This was a far better consequence than the public flogging that the students wanted. **I observed that the students would not hit back if they could trust that the person who initiated the hit would receive a consequence and that justice would prevail.**

To build trust and to teach the behaviors of the fight-free process, I conducted a behavior workshop for the students. In a school of K-6, I held one workshop for primary and one for intermediate students. My lesson plan for the workshop was as follows:

Motivate the students and get their attention by reading the book, *The Principal from the Black Lagoon* by Mike Thaler, which tells the story of a boy who was sent to the principal's office. His imagination got the better of him as he waited his turn to see the principal. He imagined that ghoulish and horrible things would happen to him while inside the office. In reality once inside the office, he stated his case and the principal told him to apologize to the teacher for accidentally removing her wig and to be more careful with the broom handle.

I then asked students to tell me the reasons why they might get sent to the office. The children participated readily and came up with the very list that I had collected from discipline forms throughout the year. I asked the students where these infractions that had led them to the office occurred and they all agreed: the cafeteria, the hallway, the playground, the restroom, and on the bus. I asked them why they did not fight in the classroom and they said, "The teacher might see us." I posed the question, "Well, do you think we really need a video camera in all these places? Do you only behave because someone is watching?" Despite what I believe about lectures, I took my chance by giving a brief lecture on the rights of individuals to come to school and be safe, and how they had a right not to be hit or harassed at school. From today on, hitting was no longer accepted as kid's stuff, just growing up, just playing around, or accidental assault. There were some things they could do to avoid fighting even though they might have become angry at something someone else had said or done.

A lesson on anger followed. An overhead of the human brain outlined the blood flow into the thinking regions of the brain. I pointed out to the students that an animal does not have this thinking region, and that the blood triggers an attack response when the animal is angered. We do not have to respond as an animal with no ability to think, and if we calm down when we are angry, we can be in control of the situation, not giving the person who angered us the power to get us in trouble. We could count to ten slowly giving our blood time to flow into the thinking region or cognitive portion of our brains. Students said their moms had told them that before, but they did not know why. "It is simply so that the blood can flow into our thinking region so that we can then think, 'I will not fight.'" I told students that they could also try saying our fight-free rule, "**KEEP HANDS, FEET, AND ALL OTHER OBJECTS TO YOURSELF.**" Saying it very slowly can be the ten seconds to keep you from fighting. After calming down, you can remove yourself from the situation or call for help or go to the teacher to report what had happened. Students said that they did not want to be tattletales, and that they did not want to tell. I asked them what their parents do when there is a disturbance in the neighborhood or if there is an accident. Students readily said that their parents would dial 911 for help. I then made the analogy of parents calling the police to students calling the teacher. This would safeguard their rights to be safe and to keep the peace in our school. Another technique they could use if they were being hassled by someone, if they felt the need for relief from the situation, was to use a Write-Not-Fight form. Teachers have these forms on their desks and students fill them out to identify who they are having a problem with and what they have tried, thus far, to solve the problem. This form then goes back to the teacher's desk, and the teacher helps the students to mediate the problems.

Another effective instructional lesson utilizes the story of the book, *The Eagles who Thought They were Chickens* by Mychal Wynn. Through the story, students examine how baby eagles who hatch in a chicken yard are ridiculed by the chickens and roosters who

Dr. Margaret R. Dolan

exclaim that they are, "dumb, ugly chickens." The baby eagles are ridiculed because of their differences. Through an analysis of the story, students identify typical behaviors around their school. Through the classroom activities, students affirm eagle language and behaviors to literally stamp out chicken language and behaviors. They add another affirmation into their behavioral arsenal when confronted with the "chicken" behaviors of others as they exclaim, "Don't be a chicken, be an eagle."

Instructional Activity

Using chart paper with the headings: playground, cafeteria, hallway, restroom, bus, and to and from school, I asked the students what a fight-free playground would look like, what it would sound like, what it would feel like? Students freely responded and we charted their examples. (Only positive samples were placed on the chart.)

Using some students as actors and actresses, we used situations that led to conflict and acted out what it looked like when you did not fight. For example, in a name-calling scenario: student A calls student B a name, student B tries ignoring the insult. Student A continues to call student B names. Student B counts to ten and walks away. Student B writes out a Write-Not-Fight form and the teacher mediates or leads the students in appropriate conversation to get the issues out in the open and to help students talk about how they will treat each other in the future. Other scenarios included butting in line, taking food off another person's tray in the cafeteria, calling a student's mom a name (e.g., "Yo mama looks like..."), making fun of shortcomings (e.g., running the mile too slowly in gym class).

Referring to these, I told the students that I would remind them of our behavior workshop and the things we learned during my morning and afternoon announcements in the future. I also told them I would report to them how many students were fight free each day reminding them of the number one rule we now have everywhere in our school, on the bus, and on the way home: **KEEP HANDS, FEET, AND ALL OTHER OBJECTS TO YOURSELF.**

> *Each morning, I would use a sample from the workshop and invite students to put a picture in their heads of how they would act today if someone butted in line and made them mad. I would recite the rule and encourage them with positive affirmations so that by the end of the day I knew we would have the 520 fight-free students we started out with.*

Each morning, I would use a sample from the workshop and invite students to put a picture in their heads of how they would act today if someone butted in line and made them angry. I would recite the rule and encourage them with positive affirmations so that by the end of the day I knew we would have the 520 fight-free students we started out with. Each day passed, and as I looked at the clock at 11:00 A.M. I would find that by 1:00 P.M., there were no fights. My office staff would cheer as I made the end of the day announcement. Students loved the cheering and the teachers noticed that the students waited to hear the report and would begin to cheer at their desks. After two weeks of no fighting, I told the students that I was so happy I would make them a flag which we would fly right under our American flag to tell the entire neighborhood that we were fight free at McNair Elementary. My feeble Betsy Ross skills found my first flag attempt shredded to pieces on the first afternoon that it flew when a storm hit our area. But remember my detention supervisor who bought a mink coat with her detention earnings? She came to the rescue and volunteered to sew another flag, designed by one of our fifth grade students.

The flag would fly every day when there was not a fight. (A fight was defined as two persons exchanging physically aggressive contact.) As mentioned before, single hits, kicks, shoves or pushes increased because students were not hitting back. Students did not want the flag to come down. To address the issue of single assaults, the code of conduct consequences were administered. In addition, the classroom ribbon came down for a day. The classroom ribbon was a large ribbon in school colors and gold lettering which read "We're a Fight-Free Classroom." These ribbons were hung outside the classroom doors. A quick glance down the hall provided a clear visual report of where there might have been a single assault. The redemption was that the ribbon came down for only one day. Admonishment or chiding the student responsible for the loss of the ribbon was not necessary as the visual symbol or lack of it did the trick. Students received individual small ribbons to wear that read, "I'm a Fight-Free Wildcat." The school superintendent came to the assembly where we unveiled our flag, classroom ribbons, and gave individual ribbons. The superintendent was amazed that the students had not had one fight, and it was October 14. We had done it. We were fight free. What would we do when we had our first fight? Not until February did our first fight occur. There were two fights that day: two boys and two girls—one set primary and one intermediate. The five of us walked to the flag and the four children took it down and put it in my office. At three o'clock, I made the following announcement: "Congratulations, boys and girls! We have 516 students who know and practice our rule: KEEP HANDS, FEET, AND ALL OTHER OBJECTS TO YOURSELF. Tomorrow, I know we will have 520 fight-free students and our flag will fly again."

By four o'clock I had a phone call from a parent whose child was upset that the flag was down. The mayor was driving by and came in to ask me if everything was all right. Did I need help? I asked him if he could come by when the flag was back up and recognize the students for not fighting. The next day, the four students who had taken the flag down, came with me to raise the flag again. The mayor came to announce that we had 520 fight-free students. The flag only came down once more that first year. My annual report read, **"No suspensions for fighting."** And there were only three fights which computed to a 94% drop in fights at McNair Elementary School.

> *By four o'clock I had a phone call from a parent whose child was upset that the flag was down. The mayor was driving by and came in to ask me if everything was all right. Did I need help? I asked him if he could come by when the flag was back up and recognize the students for not fighting. The next day, the four students who had taken the flag down, came with me to raise the flag again. The mayor came to announce that we had 520 fight-free students. The flag only came down once more that first year. My annual report read, "No suspensions for fighting."*

Dr. Margaret R. Dolan

Several built-in procedures served to keep the students motivated during that first Fight-Free Year. The school staff worked as a team to provide positive reinforcement whenever possible. For example, when it was necessary for the classroom ribbon to come down because a student in the class had used physically-aggressive behavior, the teacher did not lament to the class, "Now look what happened. I am embarrassed that our ribbon came down. I will not be able to show my face in the teachers' lounge!" Instead, teachers took the ribbons down with the encouragement that they were sure to be back up again the next day. If one student in the room seemed to be a repeater, the teacher would consult with the student offering a Fight-Free Assessment Activity and they would explore the individual contract approach–students assessing their own behavior (see Section IV, Fight-Free Assessment Activity). This is an area of intelligence, a way of being smart, that we can use to help the student to understand while they are developing it. It ties to self esteem when students discover that it is another way of being smart! Some teachers used it as an opportunity to review how well the class, as a whole, had been doing and as a discussion to reinforce the skills of walking away, seeking help, counting to ten, or using the Write-Not-Fight form to generate further discussion serving to clear the air and start a clean slate.

Another built-in opportunity to reinforce the positive, aside from the daily announcements from the main office, was a quarterly assembly. The assembly was entitled, **"The Principal's Red Carpet Assembly."** A piece of red carpet was placed down the middle of the gym floor as a runway. Each quarter, teachers nominated a student who had been a positive influence for the class, or who had performed a good deed that was notable, or who had done everyday tasks in a cheerful, positive manner. Some teachers used it as an opportunity to reward students who had shown improvement in work habits, attitudes, or

School Violence...Calming the Storm

good citizenship skills. The art, music, physical education, and library teachers also nominated a student from each grade level. Seeing all 520 students a week allowed them an opportunity to give the students a pat on the back and also allowed us to increase the number of students who went down the red carpet. Nominated students simply walked down the red carpet, while their names were announced. The principal also emphasized to the students that it took many people to work together to make our school a wonderful place. Next, teachers who had performed a task above and beyond the call of duty were given a chance to walk down the red carpet and children had an opportunity to applaud the teachers who had spent so many hours judging science fair projects, coordinating the spelling bee, or working with the school's student council. Next, the parents who had contributed time and effort in volunteer functions to help our school run smoothly were invited to take a walk down the red carpet, and students were able to see the people responsible for helping in our school's endeavors. The students eagerly applauded school volunteers for their hard work. A guest of honor presided over the Red Carpet Ceremony. The guest of honor could be a school board member, an administrator from the district office, or during Secretary's Week, it might be the superintendent's secretary. This provided the students with the big picture and they could see that people outside of our school helped us be the best school we could be. Each guest of honor commended the students for their fight-free efforts. One of our favorite guests was our city's mayor, David Farquharson, who gave the students a proclamation for being the *first* fight-free school in the United States. That thought in the students' heads served as a continual positive reinforcement and students held their heads high as a sense of pride came over their faces when reminded that they were the first. As you can see, a host of positive reinforcers served to be the backbone of the Fight-Free Schools process.

Wentzville West Elementary has a special visit from their "Life-size" KHFAAOOTY Bear.

Dr. Margaret R. Dolan

The cost of incentives was minimal. The flag was donated, the ribbons for the classrooms were $3.75 each, and the individual ribbons were 11 cents each. Cost does not have to be an obstacle when considering this process.

Briar Crest Elementary students display Fight-Free Sign and Classroom Ribbons.

I promised the students the first year that if they were successful, I would write an article and tell other people how they had become fight free. When the article was published in the ***Education St. Louis*** newspaper, inquiries began to come in. A principal from a neighboring district, whose daughter was practice teaching in my school, called to ask if I could tell him more about the flag that flies outside my school. He sent a discipline committee to talk with me and then invited me to speak to his staff. I credit Dave Knes, Principal of Briar Crest Elementary School in the Pattonville School District, with motivating me to share with other principals my fight-free story. Dave wanted his school to become fight free, and he was the first on board to encourage me to promote our process of fostering a positive school climate and culture.

CHAPTER 3
The Fight-Free School Mission

To teach the youth of today, the future leaders of our nation, appropriate interpersonal behavior skills. The focus is to provide an improved school environment which will enhance the learning process and allow our children the optimum advantage to excel in their academic careers.

— Fight-Free Schools Mission Statement

The mission statement of the Fight-Free Schools, Inc., has a great deal to do with effective school research and the creation of the environment most conducive to students being successful in the academic arena. Much of the effective schools research leads the educator to conclude that we do make a difference in the academic achievement of students. In the ERIC Research Action Brief, the implication offered there summarizes the role of the principal in creating and maintaining a climate for success:

The one person in the school who has the most influence on the establishment of the environment that will produce achievement is the principal. Establishing that environment is no small task, nor is it reducible to a simple formula. The principal who makes a difference brings to the job more than technical expertise. He or she dedicates mind, heart, and will to the achievement of one over-riding goal; the success of the student. It is this desire to see students succeed that propels the principal to set high standards, communicate those standards to teachers and students, and make sure students are rewarded for achievement and reminded of the standards if they fail. In sum, the effective principal is one who sees to it that his or her expectations for student success permeate the entire school.

University of Oregon
ERIC Clearinghouse on Educational Management, Number 20,
Eugene: December 8, 1997

Dr. Margaret R. Dolan

> There was no magic in flying the flag. Flying a flag over a school and saying, "We are now fight free," is not the answer, as one principal who embraced the fight-free idea found out. The principal called me in a frenzy on the first day of school and said, "Peggy, this flag isn't working. I've already had three fights, and I have two lunch periods to go." I am happy to report that this principal did back track, and with some planning and preparation, was able to launch a successful Fight-Free Campaign.

I had made some observations when the Fight-Free Schools process was set in motion in my school. Students were motivated to settle disputes in an alternative manner, they were proud of themselves individually and as a student body, and they were treating each other with more respect. Teachers used the fight-free talk to help students solve problems. With physical aggression and verbal assaults reduced, there was more time to teach. Teaching appropriate behavior became a natural and unforced component of the daily process of schooling. As principal, I had more time to spend with more students in a positive manner on the playground or in the cafeteria. Seeing the principal did not mean a student was in trouble. I was no longer spending time investigating fights. Parents were becoming more aware of the change in the school. One parent had warned her children at home, engaged in a bit of hands-on sibling rivalry, that, "If you are fight free at school, you are going to be fight free at home." We were carrying out our mission of having a fight-free school and indeed a positive climate was the result.

A mission statement looks good on paper, as do the lofty goals of effective schools and positive school climates. However, the task of putting the theory to practice is the challenge. The Fight-Free Schools process, for me, offered the ability to provide the success for every student that effective schools demanded. I was fulfilling my obligation of providing a safe and secure environment. There was no magic in flying the flag. Flying a flag over a school and saying, "We are now fight free," is not the answer, as one principal who embraced the fight-free idea found out. The principal called me in a frenzy on the first day of school and said, "Peggy, this flag isn't working. I've already had three fights, and I have two lunch periods to go." I am happy to report that this principal did back track, and with some planning and preparation, was able to launch a successful Fight-Free Campaign.

The Fight-Free Campaign

I encourage principals to engage the Fight-Free Schools process as they would an election campaign. The goal of election campaigns is to spread the good word to all audiences and to solicit help in working toward a common goal.

The three audiences with whom the principal is primarily concerned are teachers, students, and parents.

The Teachers

When I approached my teachers with the fight-free idea, it never occurred to me that I would have to convince them to support the process. I cannot stress how important teacher collaboration is to the success of fostering a positive and nurturing school climate and culture. In fact, I will go as far as to say that teacher collaboration is the *single most important component* of a successful fight-free campaign. My teachers were supportive and willing to talk the language of fight free, to provide the positive feedback and role modeling, and to reinforce the predetermined consequences consistently and without bias for any and all violations of our fight-free code. Most importantly, their attitudes to the children were, "You can do it; you can be fight free." This is the single positive attitude that permeated the school and that was the message that students and parents received. In planning with teachers, I shared our annual report which showed the increasing number of fights. They could readily see the need for a plan of action. The number of detentions and suspensions certainly showed that we were punishing the offenders and that we did have a code of conduct; however, I pointed out that we did not have a plan for *prevention*. One of my goals was to help students to become intrinsically motivated to choose alternative methods rather than fighting. The teachers collaborated and brainstormed for strategies to help define and achieve our goals.

Planning with Teachers

Meet with teachers and share your concerns, as a principal, for the need to address the issues of physical aggression, verbal put-downs, or any other forms of defiance and disrespect in your school. Sharing data pertaining to the number of fights, single assaults, etc., will provide an objective perspective of needs. Have teachers share their observations regarding classroom and school-wide behavior in the school. Discuss when and where physical aggression or verbal assaults occur. What is the language and behavior of students that hinder the learning process by disrupting classrooms, fostering an emotionally stressful environment, or making students apprehensive about putting forth any effort for fear of violence, rejection, or put-downs? What observations do teachers have about where physical or verbal altercations occur? Discuss why some teachers are successful in the classroom in controlling student behavior; why others are successful at nurturing positive behavior; and why others have classrooms that are seemingly out of control. Construct a statistical analysis of referrals and suspensions. Have teachers share special features of the rewards they use in the classroom when students are behaving appropriately. This list will be helpful in planning your school rewards. It will give you insight about what motivates students, e.g., for primary students it might be stickers, for intermediate students it might be free time, for junior high or high school students it might be recognition in the newsletter or school newspaper.

Give teachers time to read The Articles in the Additional Resources section. This will generate discussion in the rise of violence in society, in general, and in schools, in particular. It is important to recognize the unique qualities of each school and then set up a plan of action that teachers may work on to devise the instructional strategies for their schools. Create a time line that includes meeting with the teachers, preparing the students, classroom preparation, school assemblies (behavior workshops), and acquiring the necessary instructional materials. Develop an implementation plan and set goals. The Fight-Free Schools Action Plan in Section I outlines goals that may be adaptable to your school community. After preparation plans are met, tell the students that the program is in place and that they will earn the right to fly the flag if their school can go two weeks without fighting. Make morning and afternoon announcements congratulating students at the end of the day with the number of fight-free students. If there is a fight, report only the number of fight-free students. Do not say, "Now we cannot raise the flag." When first beginning the Fight-Free Schools process,

Dr. Margaret R. Dolan

> The Fight-Free Planning Committee should be representatives of the Multiple Intelligences Theory published by Howard Gardner in his book, Frames of Mind. By having individuals who are highly developed in each of the areas of Intelligences: Visual/Spatial; Verbal/Linguistic; Logical/Mathematical; Musical/Rhythmic; Body/Kinesthetic; and most recently, Naturalist, you are assured a multifaceted approach to instructional implementation of the program.

have a dry run and rehearse what a fight-free school looks like, sounds like, and feels like. Set an attainable goal for your dry run, e.g., ten days. When you reach the goal, plan a flag raising fight-free assembly. Have a fight-free planning committee to work out details and keep teachers informed. The Fight-Free Planning Committee should be made up of representatives of the Multiple Intelligences Theory published by Howard Gardner in his book, **Frames of Mind**. By having individuals who are highly developed in each of the areas of Intelligences: Visual/Spatial; Verbal/Linguistic; Logical/ Mathematical; Interpersonal; Intrapersonal; Musical/Rhythmic; Body/Kinesthetic; and most recently, Naturalist, you are assured a multifaceted approach to instructional implementation of the program. Keep in mind that of all of the Intelligences the two dominate Intelligences in a successful fight-free campaign are Verbal/Linguistic and Visual/Spatial. You must reinforce what you believe through your language and through visuals throughout your school community.

Students

Planning the kick-off for your Fight-Free Campaign can be fun and might put you in mind of a good old fashioned pep rally. We are rallying around the fight-free flag to promote fight-free behavior and celebrate how great our school is because of it. I have been invited to several kick-off assemblies. Each school used this opportunity to unveil their school's personalized flag for the first time. In one school, a first grade student designed the winning entry for their school's fight-free flag, and his parents were there to share in his moment of pride. Students are given their individual fight-free ribbons, certificates, or buttons. Classroom ribbons, banners, and windsocks are displayed. Some schools have cheerleaders who lead fight-free cheers. After the pledge of allegiance, a fight-free pledge is said by students. In one school, each homeroom chose a representative to bring each classroom's original fight-free pledge to the principal. At another school, all students signed a pledge personally that was displayed in the cafeteria. Invited guests can include community leaders, local celebrities, business partners, law enforcement officials (D.A.R.E. officers) and representatives from your school's parenting organization. Each school chose instructional approaches to "teach" and to inspire. Illustrating the flag; making the flag; promoting the language and behaviors; reinforcing the beliefs; internalizing and verbalizing the language and behaviors all served as instructional components to fostering a positive school climate and culture.

School Violence...Calming the Storm

St. Blaise Elementary students display their Classroom Ribbons at their Fight-Free Kick-off Assembly.

Behavior Workshop

At planning sessions with teachers, decide the best composition of assemblies for your school. Some schools prefer by grade levels; some divide by primary and intermediate; some prefer the entire school to be present (especially for smaller schools, e.g., 250 students). One principal said that he really liked the concept of "Fight Free" and wanted to become a fight-free school, but he was not Peggy Dolan and did not think he could pull off the Behavior Workshop. I asked him what he could do instead of the assembly. He said he was better at getting his ideas across to students by visiting individual classrooms. The principal then set out to introduce the fight-free concept to his students by visiting each classroom. He achieved his goal of seeing each class in September and by October, their flag was flying high.

Decide the role-modeling component and who will model your values and beliefs. I used students for modeling behavior. One school used students for situations demonstrating appropriate behavior and the teachers acted as students, role modeling inappropriate behavior. Situations for role modeling can be generated during teacher planning, students can generate the list, or the principal can choose the top ten reasons why students were engaged in fights from the discipline referrals to the office.

Dr. Margaret R. Dolan

Role Modeling Sample Situations:

A student calls another student a name.

A student makes fun of another student for poor performance in gym class.

A student makes fun of another student's mother.

A student blames another student for taking some food off his/her tray in the cafeteria.

A student butts in line.

A student threatens another student.

The instructional phase of the Behavior Workshop gives the students concrete ways to prevent a fight and serves to introduce them to the system to be used in the building when physical confrontations occur.

Defining a Fight

A fight is when two or more persons engage in physically or verbally aggressive behavior, e.g., two people hit, kick, shove, push, pinch, scratch, pull hair, bite, or engage in verbal put-downs.

Emphasize that fighting behavior will not be tolerated in your school. "Students have a right to come to school and to feel safe when they are here. We will work together to create a fight-free school where no fights or verbal put-downs will be tolerated. It is our school and being fight free will be up to us." Here are ways to remember to be fight free and use the fight-free system. The system is like the one we use in our neighborhoods. If there is a disturbance call the police. Going to the teacher or adult supervisor to report a hit is not tattling, it is keeping the peace in our school. By reporting events, we can maintain peace and thus model the system of justice.

Thinking Fight Free

An overhead of the human brain, with labels showing the functions of the brain, displays the thinking section of the human brain. The presentation will explain that animals do not have this thinking section.

> *"We will work together to create a fight-free school where no fights or verbal put-downs will be tolerated. It is our school and being fight free will be up to us." Here are ways to remember to be fight free and use the fight-free system. The system is like the one we use in our neighborhoods. If there is a disturbance call the police. Going to the teacher or adult supervisor to report a hit is not tattling, it is keeping the peace in our school.*

When animals meet with threatening situations they attack because their brain does not have a place for the blood to flow that will allow them to think their way out of a situation. As blood flows through the brain, it first flows to the emotion section where we see the word anger. When you become angry your blood is in this section of your

School Violence...Calming the Storm

brain. If you stop and count to ten or slowly say our fight-free rule to yourself, you will give your blood time to flow to the section of your brain that is the thinking section. You will not act on instinct or impulse as an animal. You do not have to attack like the animal does. You can stop and think clearly about the situation and come to a solution. You can report the person who made you angry, especially if they have hurt you physically. By hitting back, we create a fighting situation. If you do not hit back, there is no fight. The person who hit first will pay a consequence according to our code of conduct. That person has the problem now, you do not. And, you have kept the school fight free. If the person continues to bother you, verbally, and you still think you want to hit them to make them stop, use a Write-Not-Fight form. These forms will be on your teachers' desks. You may fill it out and give it back to the teacher. He or she will then help you with alternative solutions to fighting and will help mediate the situation. Walking away from a person who is threatening you will help you at the moment, and telling the teacher will help you down the road.

You may not see the results of the enforced consequences and you may think, "That boy hit me and he didn't get into trouble." In our system, all students who do not keep hands, feet, and all other objects to themselves will pay consequences and that will be the principal's job. We all have a job to do in our Fight-Free System.

The other job I will have is reporting to you every day how many students in our school are fight free. We will start each day with everyone being fight free and at the end of the school day, we will announce that same number because I know that when we work together, we can do this. The teachers have promised to do their jobs, I know you will do yours, and I promise to do mine. In fact, we will fly a fight-free flag each day that we are fight free. Our classrooms will display classroom ribbons each day that they are fight free. Let us say someone kicks you going down the stairs and you do not kick back. You report the kick, I will investigate, and the homeroom for the student who kicked will have to take their ribbon down for a day.

Acting as a Fight-Free Role Model

"We have some sample situations of students in a possible fighting situation. We will act out, first, what it would be if the two students do not fight and secondly how it would be if the two students did fight." Teachers can work with the students to create scenarios and examples (see sample in Role Playing in Section II).

Communicate your goal. For example, "When we can have ten consecutive days without a single fight, we will raise our fight-free flag. Now let's talk about places in, and on the way to and from the school where we seem to have fights most often." *Display large pieces of paper labeled: cafeteria, hallway, restroom, playground, bus, and on the way to and from school.* "Now let's brainstorm and you tell me how we can become fight free. What does a fight-free cafeteria look like?" *Have students share descriptions and list on paper.* "What does a fight-free cafeteria sound like?" Again, list responses. "What does a fight-free cafeteria feel like?" *Follow this format for each area labeled.*

Dr. Margaret R. Dolan

Consider having a fight-free flag design contest in art classes. In homerooms create fight-free pledges like the pledge to the United States of America flag. When you fly your flag for the first time, have an assembly to celebrate and sing your fight-free song. Have your parents or PTA purchase each student their very own fight-free ribbon to wear each day or to your special fight-free assemblies throughout the year. Communicate your "I know you can do it, we can be fight free" belief to your entire school community.

Sample Fight-Free Role Model Scenario

First sample are when two students use the fight-free system.

Student A: "Hey, you butted in line. You do it all the time and I'm sick of it."

Student B: "I was here in this place in line everyday this week, and I'm going to be here tomorrow."

Student A: "I was here first today, and it doesn't matter where you were all week."

Student B: "I don't care what you think. Do you want to see who is stronger? I'll keep my place whenever I want because I could beat you up with one hand tied behind my back."

The line begins to move and the teacher who was talking with another student facing the opposite direction is now ready to take the students to their homeroom.

Once in the homeroom, student A goes to the desk for a **Write-Not-Fight Form** proceeding to fill it out and places it back on the teacher's desk.

The teacher reads the form and calls student A and B together and they talk out a workable agreement, reinforcing the inappropriate behavior of butting in line, reporting the threat by student B on a discipline referral form, and thanking student A for using the form to help solve the problem instead of fighting.

Scenario:

Student A shoves Student B out of line and Student B comes back to push Student A. Teacher intervenes, telling students A and B that a discipline referral for fighting will go to the office and the teacher takes down the classroom ribbon.

Students A and B are with the principal who asks, "What rule did you break? You did not keep hands, feet, and all other objects to yourself. This is a first offense for both of you, and you will serve detention hours. I will be calling your parents. Right now you can go with me to the flag to take it down." After taking the flag down, the principal says, "Now, Student A and Student B, I'll see you tomorrow, first thing, and you can help me raise the flag."

Principal's rule: Always have the students who take the flag down help you raise the flag the next day.

School Violence...Calming the Storm

Parents

Including parents in planning can be a great benefit for the long-term success of the fight-free process. Parental support is needed to encourage the common Fight-Free language. Some parents are reluctant to say, "Don't hit back," or "Go tell an adult if you are hassled." Some will say, "Oh, I don't want to tell my child to tattletale," or "If my child gets hit they have my permission to hit back." Every parent will agree that every child has a right to come to school and not be hassled, harassed, or hit. A school's environment should be a safety zone. That zone has been invaded by the increase in violence in our nation. To ensure a safety zone for students, a principal can present Fight Free as a system to maintain a safe environment for children to achieve academically. Sharing the concept at a PTA/PTO meeting or an introductory letter informs parents of the expectations of the school. Showing a Fight-Free video of results at other schools is a powerful and constructive motivational tool for inspiring parents to consider Fight Free as a viable alternative to fostering a positive and nurturing school climate and culture.

One year I conducted a "Forum on Violence" for parents and invited law enforcement personnel, our mayor, and other experts to serve on a panel about such issues as gangs, safety on the way to and from school, and Neighborhood Watch Programs. A contract was signed by parents, the mayor, our D.A.R.E. officer, students, and the principal as a pledge to educate ourselves on the issues violence proposes. Including Fight-Free news in your school newsletter provides an ongoing avenue to keep parents up to date on the Fight-Free process at your school. Parents, through their PTA/PTO, can offer support by funding incentives. One PTA purchased a Disney Site License and once a month the principal shows Disney movies to the fight-free students in attendance. Money for the school flag, classroom flag or banners, individual buttons, ribbons, or medallions for each student can be provided by the PTA/PTO.

One parent approached me at the beginning of our fight-free efforts and said she really did not like the Fight-Free Flag flying because people will think we have a "bad school." She turned her thinking around when I thanked her for being an avid supporter of the Drug-Free Program. Just as the Drug-Free Banner was supporting drug education as a preventative measure, so too was the Fight-Free Flag flying to prevent fights and to announce to the community that we had no fights here today.

> *One parent approached me at the beginning of our fight-free efforts and said she really did not like the Fight-Free Flag flying because people will think we have a "bad school." She turned her thinking around when I thanked her for being an avid supporter of the Drug-Free Program. Just as the Drug-Free Banner was supporting drug education as a preventative measure, so too was the Fight-Free Flag flying to prevent fights and to announce to the community that we had no fights here today.*

Dr. Margaret R. Dolan

While on a local radio talk show on KMOX radio, the commentator, Barbara Whiteside, asked me if I could come up with a Fight-Free family concept so that her boys would quit squabbling. That year, our PTA sponsored a Fight-Free Families Program which promoted a family meeting to discuss where siblings do the most squabbling, consequences for squabbling, and designing their own Fight-Free Family Flag to fly on the refrigerator. One of the key components of this process is the family meeting. As a child, my parents held the family meeting every evening at 6:00 P.M.–that was supper time. Ed and Della Dolan held court, reviewing news of the day, conduct in school, and generally letting their expectations be known for things like: fights on the way home from school, making faces at the teacher, etc. Some parents today say that they do not have time for family meals because of working, sports, scouts, etc. Sometimes being caught up in the "busyness" of life leaves the business of life unattended. Somewhere between daycare, school, sports, and busy schedules, we fail to talk to our children. So who is giving them the behavior lessons they need to know? Television? Pop music? Friends? Maybe no one! Exploring reasons for the increase in violence by our youth, one reason given is the double working-parent family. Ed and Della Dolan both worked; however, every night at 6:00 P.M., we all had supper together and would not have thought of being late. So working parents or stay-at-home parents, one thing is for certain: the need to talk to children and share the expectations of behavior and the consequences of inappropriate behavior. Television watching would not be so harmful if parents were aware of, and talked about, what their children were watching. Trusting the teaching of behavior lessons to the television is risky business. Do the children imitate the violent scenes shown in cartoons, videos, or the movies? Talking about what the children are watching on television presupposes that the parents are watching with their children. This is an excellent opportunity to talk about the way people treat each other and offers a perfect forum for talking about expectations with children. The **Fight-Free Parent Handbook** can be a great tool for parents to stimulate discussions about positive language and behavior. It also provides a framework to support parents in their efforts to teach their children positive language and positive behavior toward each person in their households.

> *One of the key components of this process is the family meeting. As a child, my parents held the family meeting every evening at 6:00 P.M.–that was supper time. Ed and Della Dolan held court, reviewing news of the day, conduct in school, and generally letting their expectations be known for things like: fights on the way home from school, making faces at the teacher, etc. Some parents today say that they do not have time for family meals because of working, sports, scouts, etc. Sometimes being caught up in the "busyness" of life leaves the business of life unattended. Somewhere between daycare, school, sports, and busy schedules, we fail to talk to our children.*

CHAPTER 4
Launching the Fight-Free Program

The first day our grand banner came down, several parents came into the school while dropping off their children to see if everything was all right in the school, and why the banner had come down.

— McNair Elementary School Parent

Students can readily identify with the components of a campaign. In launching the Fight-Free Campaign, we fashioned the presentation of our message by using every campaign method we knew (remember, the Multiple Intelligences application). Flags waving, ribbons bearing our message, buttons, bumper stickers, t-shirts, rallies, and the like all served to keep the fight-free momentum going. Each school must decide what language, visual incentives, etc., based on the unique school culture and students it serves that will be effective in serving as motivational tools. However, every school that develops a Fight-Free Plan has one thing in common and that is the Fight-Free flag, or as one school called it, "The Grand Banner." Flying the school's Fight-Free Flag under the American flag or showcasing it in a highly visible location will serve as the announcement to all that the school is fight free. Some schools have held flag design contests and unveiled the winning design at their kick-off fight-free rally. (See Appendix for flag details.) The flag flies every day that there is not a fight. ***A fight consists of two persons engaging in physically aggressive contact.*** The persons who engage in the fight are the ones who take the flag down when the fight occurs. The same two persons meet the principal the next morning to raise the flag themselves. This dynamic serves as a motivational tool, clearly and purposefully teaching that each choice (engage in fighting or verbally-abusive behavior) is accompanied by consequences and displays the personal responsibility and empowerment that is involved in the Fight-Free Schools process. The students are the main determiners of the flag flying. Students reason quickly that if they do not hit back, then it is not a fight. What happens then if one person hits, kicks, shoves, pushes, bites, scratches, or verbally assaults another person? The dynamic here is that the classroom or homeroom ribbon of the person who chooses to engage in a single assault on another is taken down for a day. Each room has an individual ribbon stating that they are a fight-free classroom. The classroom ribbon will go back up the next day. Some schools have used other symbols for the classrooms or homerooms such as windsocks designed for their rooms or banners or pennant type flags. Principals say that many a dreary hallway has been brightened due to the presence of the flags. Students are proud when walking the hallways and have yet another visual reminder of how great their school is doing. Remember, this is an wholistic endeavor and we are making every attempt to stimulate the senses through fostering our positive, nurturing school climate and culture.

Dr. Margaret R. Dolan

> *Children become fight free by learning "how" to be fight free. Children must be taught that language is their primary vehicle for resolving conflicts. When children learn the words, practice restraint, and develop patience then fight-free problem solving will become as natural as saying, "Good morning."*
>
> **Dr. Terre Butler**
> **Director, The Proficiency in English Program Los Angeles Unified Schools**

The team approach of "all for one" is utilized at this point. When the classroom ribbon or banner is taken down, there is no chiding of the student by teacher or students. Sometimes nothing is said at all. Taking down the classroom symbol has said it all. Teachers might offer words of encouragement, stating that even though the flag is down today it will be back in its place tomorrow, and that we will all work together to keep it flying. Perhaps the next morning as it goes up, the teacher can review alternatives to aggressiveness when conflicts arise. This is also a good opportunity to discuss the appropriate social skills that were discussed in the behavior workshop. Fight-Free activities integrated into instructional lessons throughout the school year provide a means for making the Fight-Free message meaningful, relevant, and real-life rather than an abstract concept.

Some staff and parents become concerned about the impact of the behavior of one student penalizing the whole classroom. Remember, the only student with a penalty is the one who chose to hit or verbally put down another student, who is now paying the consequences for his or her actions as stipulated in the code of conduct. The group's symbol coming down is a means of keeping score and a visual symbol of their tally for the day. Individual incentives continue to hold the individual student responsible and the individual incentives of one student are not taken away due to the inappropriate behavior of another student. The analogy of one person's choices having an affect on society is effective when explaining the reasoning behind the classroom or school flag coming down. However, no one but the individual can take away individual incentive. My school has adopted different individual incentives each year. One year, we had simple ribbons pinned to the student that said, "I'm a Fight-Free Student." Some of the younger students would lose their ribbons, so some teachers held them and students donned them at our quarterly assemblies or at times designated by the teacher. Another year, our parents made Fight-Free Buttons for each student with the flag on it. In another year, the slogan, "Keep Hands, Feet, and All Other Objects to Yourself" appeared on the button. Most recently we have adopted medallions for each student, worn around their necks at each quarterly assembly if the student was fight free. At the close of the school year, students who remained fight free the entire year, could take the medallions home.

Government participation comes into play for incentives. Each year, our County Executive, Mr. Buzz Westfall, gives participating schools a certificate and schools can duplicate certificates for each student who is fight free. This form of recognition serves as a motivator and plants the seed for others in the next year so that they, too, can earn a certificate by keeping hands, feet, and all other objects to themselves.

Behind the flag and classroom ribbon concept is a firm and fair code of conduct that requires consistent administration of consequences. The flag and the ribbons serve as visual reinforcements and the code of conduct serves as the system of justice. Students only learn to trust that the system is in play when it is equitably and consistently enforced. Without the teacher having to report the consequences, students know that when a ribbon or flag comes down the consequences stipulated in the ***Code of Conduct Book*** will be administered. It is wise for each school to have a code of conduct that students, parents, and teachers are aware of, and can rely upon. There should be a consequence for any verbal put-downs or hands-on aggressive behavior. While many would argue that name-calling is innocent and natural, it is a hindrance to the educational process and contributes to a negative and disruptive classroom culture. Name-calling in its most innocent form is hurtful emotionally to those who are the recipients of the verbal abuse. In its more insidious forms it promotes biases, stereotypes, and prejudices that escalate to more frequent verbal attacks, eventual physical attacks or retaliation, and most tragically, beatings, stabbings, shootings or other more deadly forms of physical assaults. There is nothing unnatural about children being taught how to be kind, considerate, and encouraging to one another.

Nearly all school districts have established an expected Code of Conduct which outlines the consequences for physical transgressions. A first offense may result in detention. A second offense may result in suspension from school. However, punishing does not root out the behavior. Behavior frequently reveals itself in negative language and put-downs long before the physical transgression occurs. The Fight-Free process is designed to change the core behavior, how we treat each other, before it explodes in violence. Teaching the appropriate social skills, increases consciousness, and leads to more positive choices.

Several issues arise once you set out on your fight-free course. Students will tell you, "We were just playing around," or "We only pushed; it was play fighting," or "We talk about each other all of the time. We don't really mean it." Articulate from the start that these excuses are not acceptable, period. Set high expectations and be diligent and consistent in reinforcing your expectations.

Another issue that one school reported was that the same students consistently caused the flag to come down. I suggested to the school that they take the problem back to the students and talk about solutions. The students reasoned that these students should be not only suspended from school but suspended from the Fight-Free campaign. It seemed that the repeat offenders had power over the flag and were misusing their power. Since they did not value the fight-free system, they should not be a part of it. Upon their return to school, they were given a fight-free behavior session with the counselor and were told that they would have to earn their way back into their Fight-Free school. Terms were worked out and by the end of

Dr. Margaret R. Dolan

the next month, these students had rejoined their classmates for the fight-free pizza party. One rule of thumb for repeat offenders could be the "three strikes and you're out" rule. The repeater is removed from the Fight-Free ranks and placed on a behavior contract until his/her good behavior earns re-enrollment into Fight Free. Generally, if for the second fight a student is suspended, there is not usually a third. Remember a code of conduct works with the flag.

The issue of problem-solving is a critical factor in this process. Principals will call and ask if what they are doing is right or wrong. I always respond with the question, "Is it working for you? Are you getting the results you want?" Then it is right. Remember, each school exists at different points along the process of change. Each school community has an unique socioeconomic and cultural make-up. Each school will have to tailor the plan to meet the unique needs of its school community. If it seems that something is not working, then pinpointing the problem and seeking alternative solutions will help. One principal called after beginning the process and said that the kindergarten students were having a terrible adjustment to this. The principal had to suspend kindergartners and the teachers were complaining that this process does not work for young children. Remember, I stated earlier that teacher collaboration is critical to the success of this process. It goes without saying that teacher beliefs affect their willingness to collaborate. Our beliefs influence our expectations. Do we believe that our kindergarten students can be fight free? Do we believe that our poor students can be fight free? Do we believe that the students who come to us from single-parent households can be fight free? Do we believe that our LD, LDHD, or our students who have been identified by any number of labels or acronyms can be fight free? In helping the principal reflect, we were reminded that one of the lead questions posed to me during initial inquiries about the the fight-free process was the concern that kindergarten teachers did not think it would work. Aha! Beliefs. This concern grew into a problem as they attempted to implement their fight-free plan. Perhaps the teachers at this point needed more role modeling for how to teach behavior expectations, or how to talk the fight-free language. The principal decided to take the problem back to the kindergarten teachers through more of a problem-solving approach.

> *Attitude is a key factor in the success of this process. While visiting one school's staff for an orientation to Fight Free, I was greeted by at least four of the teachers who told me that the Fight-Free Program sounded good. They understood that it worked in other schools, but that I did not understand their students. They said that their students could not keep from fighting.*

Attitude is a key factor in the success of this process. While visiting one school's staff for an orientation to Fight Free, I was greeted by at least four of the teachers who told me that the Fight-Free process sounded good. They understood, it worked in other schools, but that I did not understand their students. They said, "Our students cannot keep from fighting; that is the way they are." During my session with the teachers, I shared with them some of the questions people asked me about Fight Free. One of the questions is always, "How did you get your staff to buy into this program?" My response, in all honesty, is it never occurred to me that the staff would not want the same goal I had for students. Besides, in their classrooms, they were already promoting the tenets of the Fight-Free process in their daily expectations of students. What the Fight-Free process did was to extend those same expectations to areas

Peggy Dolan with KHFAAOOTY Bear outside of a Fight-Free classroom

outside the classroom, e.g., the hallway, the restroom, cafeteria, and the playground. It was not surprising when the principal of that school called me after they had begun attempting Fight-Free, expressing that when a fight occurred, these teachers insisted that the process did not work. I encouraged the principal to concentrate on all the students who did not fight and to be diligent in his efforts. The principal worked with the staff by grade levels to solve problems and delivered the message that even if a fight occurs, there are only two people involved. Count all of the students who did not fight. Through his diligence and determination, he successfully affected what his staff believed about their student population. They have had measurable success with Fight Free.

Do rewards erode intrinsic motivation?

Receiving praise or recognition will not necessarily erode intrinsic motivation. The student knows that the reward is not the only reason for the behavior. If a teacher smiles at, praises, or gives a certificate to a student, that recognition can be perceived as a message from the teacher to the child: "I really appreciate the work you are doing." And the child may conclude, "I get to do what I really enjoy doing, and the teacher supports me, too."

– Spencer Kagan
Cooperative Learning

Dr. Margaret R. Dolan

CHAPTER 5

Government

We must stand strong for our children and that's called 'setting an example.' As County Executive of a thriving metropolitan area, it is my responsibility to join ranks with parents, teachers, and police officers to stand strong against today's escalating violence. I'm proud to promote the Ticket-To-Peace concept. It is a new and important addition to the Fight-Free School Program. I ask parents everywhere to respond to the tickets as though they were a child's cry for help. If we are vigilant for peace, violence will die of neglect.

– Buzz Westfall
St. Louis County Executive

After being encouraged to share the Fight-Free Schools Plan with other principals, I realized that it was a perfect opportunity to include the government in my efforts. Government leaders were looking for solutions to the rising violence that seemed to be growing in epidemic proportions. I approached St. Louis County Executive, Buzz Westfall. After listening to my description of the Fight-Free Plan, he had a question about the incentives–the use of Fight-Free ribbons or buttons. He was thinking about his school days and offered that if he wore a ribbon the other kids would call him a sissy, and it would probably start a fight. My response led me to the campaign concept of the Fight-Free Plan. In a campaign there are banners, flags, ribbons, and buttons. I reminded Mr. Westfall that there were buttons with his picture on it during his last election. After a few more questions he said he would like to support this process but wanted to see if there was an interest in it or if it just sounded good for my school. So he sponsored a breakfast and invited principals from throughout the St. Louis area. The response at the breakfast was overwhelming and from that breakfast meeting, principals enrolled in the Fight-Free program. It has now grown to a nationwide effort. The County Executive sponsors the newsletter, **The Fight-Free Front**. He offered a certificate to each Fight-Free School. At the first Fight-Free Night at the Ball Park, Mr. Westfall presented a proclamation to Fight Free before the 6,000 students who attended the St. Louis Cardinals' baseball game. Mr. Westfall was instrumental in acquiring the 6,000 baseball tickets that principals could use as incentives for fight-free students. To further support this process, County Executive Westfall accompanied me on a radio talk show and fielded questions about the process and its success in reducing violence in schools. Through his office, a proposal I had written to seek presidential recognition for students who are fight free was forwarded to Congressman Dick Gephardt. As you read the letter from Congressman Gephardt, you will see that government support of this instructional process to reduce violence is benefiting the students who will be our citizens of the future.

THE WHITE HOUSE
WASHINGTON

July 3, 1996

Dear Mr. Leader:

Thank you for writing to inform me of the success of the Fight-Free Schools Program. I concur that efforts to reduce violence among young people are much needed across our Nation. The Program's record in reducing the number of physical and verbal fights is impressive and I commend their work.

I also agree that appropriate national recognition should be provided to promising programs such as these and have requested that Secretary of Education, Richard Riley, explore ways this can be accomplished and respond to you directly.

Thanks for taking an interest in this important program. I look forward to continuing our work together in an effort to make America a safer place for children.

Sincerely,

Bill Clinton

The Honorable Richard A. Gephardt
Democratic Leader
House of Representatives
Washington, D.C. 20515

Dr. Margaret R. Dolan

I encourage principals to seek support of their mayors, congressmen, and governors. When they get involved, results happen. One school, in Shiloh, Illinois, invited their congressman to their kick-off assembly. The congressman could not attend so he sent a United States flag that had flown over the Capitol in Washington, DC. The students were thrilled. I have seen students sit taller when the mayor of their city comes to commend them for their fight-free efforts.

The "Crime Summit," conducted by Congressman Gephardt and the Justice Department, was an excellent opportunity to inform our government leaders of the work of Fight Free. During this time, Congress was working on the Crime Bill. The Crime Bill was being written to offer money to inner-city schools located in areas plagued by high-crime rates. My attempt as a panel member was to share the findings that violence in schools was not just an inner-city problem. While much of the money to reduce violence in schools was targeted for "high-crime rate inner-city areas," my school was not located in the

St. Louis County Executive, Buzz Westfall and Dr. Dolan display a Ticket-To-Peace.

inner city; yet, in a neighboring subdivision, a ten-year-old was abducted and killed. With the low cost of implementing a Fight-Free Plan, it was a good thing not to wait for the money from the Crime Bill that would most likely not come our way. Congressman Gephardt became an avid supporter of Fight Free and wrote a letter to President Bill Clinton to support a proposal to seek presidential recognition of fight-free behavior for students similar to the presidential support for academic and physical fitness. This would bring recognition to the students, which is a natural motivator for them. I encourage schools to call on their mayors to support their Fight-Free implementation in a variety of ways. Mayor David Farquharson of the City of Hazelwood, Missouri, presided over a flag-raising ceremony for Fight Free and offered the school a proclamation for being the **"First Fight-Free School in the United States of America."** He encouraged students each time he spoke to them and would come periodically to make announcements on the public address system. Mayor James Eagan of Florissant, Missouri, an avid supporter of Fight Free spoke at a ceremony to introduce the "Ticket-To-Peace" to students.

St. Louis County Chief of Police, Colonel Ron Battelle joins Dr. Dolan at the Ticket-To-Peace Assembly.

I encourage principals to seek support of their mayors, congressmen, and governors. When they get involved, results happen. One school, in Shiloh, Illinois, invited their congressman to their kick-off assembly. The congressman could not attend so he sent a United States flag that had flown over the Capitol in Washington, DC. The students were thrilled. I have seen students sit taller when the mayor of their city comes to commend them for their fight-free efforts. At Sperring Middle School in the Lindbergh School District, the assistant principal arranges each week to have the team fight-free scores announced by a guest announcer. Congressman Gephardt read scores one day. The Governor of Michigan nominated the first Fight-Free School in Grand Rapids, Michigan, for a community service award. This school's success has motivated other schools in the area to become fight free. Texas Attorney General Morris, included Fight Free in a manual of violence prevention programs that he has made available to the schools in his state.

Children are programmed by nature to absorb knowledge easily and joyfully when surrounded by a positive learning climate.
– Dr. Thomas Armstrong
Awakening Your Child's Natural Genius

Dr. Margaret R. Dolan

CHAPTER 6
Law Enforcement

"Okay, Warden, fly this Fight-Free Flag over your prisons and your prisoners won't fight."

– Dr. Peggy Dolan, at the
124th Congress of Correction

Since implementing Fight Free at my own school and helping scores of other schools implement their own fight-free plans, I have found law enforcement agencies to be 100% supportive and willing to provide assistance in helping to spread the Fight-Free word. Police officers from a variety of states contacted me after reading about Fight Free in the **Safe School Magazine.** Through the law enforcement inquiries, they shared with me their roles in working with students in schools. Some are resource personnel in schools and are always seeking ways to provide prevention strategies. Colonel Ron Battelle of the St. Louis County Police offered his video unit to produce a video of the Fight-Free Plan for use as an instructional tool at seminars. D.A.R.E. officers have served as guest speakers at Fight-Free Kick-Off Assemblies and spread the Fight-Free message during their lessons. In August, 1994, I was invited to speak at the 124th Congress of Correction, which is the conference for the American Correctional Association. At the first request, I was hesitant to accept after I was informed that the audience would include law enforcement personnel, wardens, drug rehabilitation personnel, juvenile officers, and so on. I expressed my uneasiness at standing before wardens with my Fight-Free flag as an elementary school principal, announcing that if they would fly a flag, their prisoners would be intrinsically motivated not to fight in prisons. The person who invited me said that he had heard me on our local radio station, KMOX, and he wanted others to know of the prevention aspect of the program and how it reduces fights in schools. Apprehensively, I accepted. When I arrived at the presentation site, I took a few minutes to walk through the exhibit hall. On a rack of books, I found a book entitled, **Prisoner's Workbook**. As I leafed through the book, I found a page that caught my eye–a page on anger control. The page had a space for the prisoner's name and places to fill in blank questions such as: "I am angry when... When I am angry I... The time of day I am most angry is... Things that make me angry... What I can do instead of fighting..." This page looked exactly like the Write-Not-Fight form we use for Fight-Free Schools. I suddenly realized why I was there and began my talk to the wardens by showing them the similarities between the prisoner's workbook page on anger and the student's Write-Not-Fight form. We both, basically, have the same job, only at different ends of the spectrum. This made me realize the importance of teaching alternatives to violent, aggressive behavior at an early age. Perhaps more emphasis at an early age would mean fewer prisoners at an older age.

Members of the Missouri Police Juvenile Officers Association awarded me the MPJOA "Hall of Fame Award" which is presented to a citizen contributing service above and beyond the call of duty for children. They have included Fight Free in their presentations at conferences and have been supportive in spreading the Fight-Free message.

The police chiefs supported the program 100 percent when they became a part of the Ticket-To-Peace Program. This program is an extension of the Fight-Free Plan which highlights the Write-Not-Fight concept. The Ticket-To-Peace was designed after hearing about a six-year-old girl who had stabbed a ten-year-old girl on the way home from school because she became increasingly upset that the older girl kept pushing her. The six-year-old ran home and retrieved a kitchen knife from the drawer and stabbed the older girl. The St. Louis newspaper quoted the mother of the six-year-old as saying that she tells all of her kids to take care of themselves however they have to. After thinking that if only the six-year-old girl had felt that someone would listen to her, she could have solved the problem with help. I created a Ticket-To-Peace that can be used by any school or by any child. Being in a Fight-Free School is not a requirement for using the ticket. The ticket includes, inside the peace symbol, words from parents, principal, and police. Students are encouraged to write a problem they are having with someone on the ticket and give the ticket to their parent, principal, or local police. These people can help.

Former City of St. Louis Police Chief, Clarence Harmon, and St. Louis County Police Chief, Colonel Ron Battelle, supported the Ticket-To-Peace and supplied a quotation for the brochure. Colonel Battelle came to our school to launch the program in the St. Louis area.

Some junior and middle high schools use the Ticket-To-Peace in each classroom as their Write-Not-Fight form. In Michigan, Chief Hagarty of Grand Rapids, paid for Sibley School's flag and supports the program as a resource policeman in the school. Resource police are quick to use the Fight-Free program as a preventative measure to get the non-violent message across.

Community and Business Participation

Business response to schools has been instrumental in supplying incentives for schools and funding seminars so that school personnel could receive training. In St. Louis, the St. Louis Cardinals Baseball Team has supplied 6,000 tickets over the past three years to Fight-Free Schools in the city and county. An advertising firm, Gannett Advertising, donated a billboard to announce Fight-Free Day at the Ball Park, and they have promised the use of another billboard for the cause when we need it. We have slated October's **Week Without Violence Program** to proclaim the Fight-Free Schools in St. Louis. Stiffel Nickols, an accounting firm in St. Louis, sponsors seminars for Fight-Free Schools; because of their support, the word has spread throughout Missouri and to national conferences. A Subway Sandwich Shop manager donated Subway sandwiches to the winning Fight-Free team at a middle school. Another middle school was allowed the use of the recreation center in their community for students who had earned the reward day by being peaceful students in school.

The support of the news media has resulted in recognition for students and shares the success stories of Fight-Free Schools so that other schools will be inspired to set high

Dr. Margaret R. Dolan

expectations for their students. Radio stations have included Fight Free on talk shows. KMOV - TV supported the Ticket-To-Peace plan by making commercials with students explaining the concept. Our educational television station, KETC, hosted a show highlighting the program and interviewed several students who conveyed a strong message to other students. Schools now send me their articles from across the nation when their schools receive coverage. The success stories are contagious and have chronicled the program thus far.

I had a great feeling of relief when I began to understand that a youngster needs more than just subject matter. I know mathematics well, and I teach it well. I used to think that was all I needed to do. Now I teach children, not math. I accept the fact that I can only succeed partially with some of them. When I don't have to know all the answers, I seem to have more answers than when I tried to be the expert.

– Everet Shostrom
Man, The Manipulator

CHAPTER 7
Most Often-Asked Questions about the Fight-Free Schools Program

Radio appearances and workshop presentations have yielded a set of the most asked questions of Fight Free which might help others in their beginning stages.

1. What about parents who give their children permission to fight and encourage them to do so if the child has been hit?

ANSWER

A principal's response to a parent who insists that his or her child can fight should focus on a number of issues. One issue is that in a society where violence is on the increase and children at a younger age are resorting to using weapons, namely knives or guns when becoming angry, when their child aggressively engages in a conflict with another child, the other child might have a knife or gun. The repercussions of that could be fatal in the worst scenario or could disable their child for life. Therefore, using the system in place, seeking help and depending on justice being served in the administration of a code of conduct will keep their child safe. Another issue is that when the code of conduct is administered, it is administered to all students involved in the aggressive conflict and the consequences of his or her child fighting, whatever the motivation, will result in his or her child having to serve the consequences as well. Presenting the *total* picture of a safe environment in a school as a right and empowering all students with the responsibility to keep the school environment safe would be a better lesson for responsibility in solving the problem. Hitting back only compounds the problem and does not solve. it.

2. In Fight-Free Schools, if the flag comes down, why should all the kids suffer for what two students did?

ANSWER

The Fight-Free Flag flies as a symbol that there are no fights in our school today and is a visual means for keeping score. Students will be reminded when the flag does come down that they still maintain their individual Fight-Free status.

Dr. Margaret R. Dolan

> *Effectively dealing with the behaviors that cause classroom disruptions and that result in physical or emotional harm to other students early help to nurture a positive school climate and culture that ultimately contributes to a more rewarding learning environment for all students. Enforcing the Code of Conduct consistently will yield the expected results in behavior.*

3. What if the same students are responsible for repeatedly taking down the flag?

ANSWER

First of all, after the second offense, students not only cause the fight-free flag to come down, but they are suspended from school. In most cases this deters the repeated behavior. However, should a student continue, then our "three strikes and you are out" rule applies. A third time will result in the students' removal from the fight-free program and being placed on an individual behavior contract. This will work toward the student's improved behavior and re-entry into the fight-free program after a given period. (Four to six weeks is a suitable time for the student to work on the contract with the counselor and parents.)

4. How about the kindergarten and primary students? After all, they are just kids. Are they held to the same zero tolerance of hitting and name-calling? Kids will be kids.

ANSWER

The earlier the lesson of zero tolerance is learned, the more the students will adhere to the fight-free expectations of keeping hands, feet, and all other objects to themselves. (A longer period of rehearsing and including them in the program is an option. However, in most schools the expectation is across the board, and the impulsive behavior of the younger student becomes a way to instruct them on the appropriate behavior.) Effectively dealing with the behaviors that cause classroom disruptions and that result in physical or emotional harm to other students early help to nurture a positive school climate and culture that ultimately contributes to a more rewarding learning environment for all students. Enforcing the Code of Conduct consistently will yield the expected results in behavior. The behavior workshop, lessons included in daily announcements and class discussion time, are ways to continually reinforce our expectations and will help students internalize positive behaviors leading to positive life choices. Everyone has a right to come to school and not be verbally or physically assaulted; this begins when they enter the school door. 'Kids will be kids' is not a slogan for inappropriate behavior nor is it an excuse for accepting it.

5. What about the behavior disordered? The ADD, the ADHD, the LD? Are they in the Fight-Free program?

ANSWER

ALL STUDENTS ARE A PART OF THE FIGHT-FREE PROCESS! This proactive preventative approach gives students with disabilities alternatives to inappropriate behavior. Once they see that the expectations are the same for all, this is one area where they are not different any more. In my school, there is a room for behavior disordered students and they are the first to use the Write-Not-Fight form or the system of seeking help because they are not always the perpetrators. If a bully uses disabled students as a target or makes fun of them, they feel that in this system they will be heard. Therefore, they do not have to take matters into their own hands by hitting. Everyone speaks the same language.

6. What if there are negative teachers on staff, and they believe that the students are not capable of being fight free?

ANSWER

There will always be those who see the glass as half empty. Now that so many schools of varying demographic and socioeconomic backgrounds have tried the program and have been successful, then data can be presented to pave a more positive road. The Fight-Free process appeals to the need for a safe school environment that all teachers realize, and offers this as a strategy. Include negative-minded teachers in the planning process, rely on the power of the "positive" being as contagious as the "negative," and educate to solicit more people in the ranks.

7. Do you think this process uses peer pressure in the wrong way?

ANSWER

An example of peer pressure used in the wrong way would be a member of any of the hundreds of violent U.S. street gangs. The Fight-Free Gang places a different value on appropriate behavior and makes it cool not to fight. Let's face it, anyone who knows anything about children knows that peer pressure and the the need to belong are powerful motivators to children. Rather than allowing negative peer pressure to influence our school community, we rely on positive peer pressure to help us to nurture the school climate and culture. Any time you have humans interacting, you will observe peer pressure. This proactive approach does not leave the results to chance. We choose to teach appropriate behavior and make known high expectations, giving us positive results by using peer pressure to our advantage.

8. Why do we have to reward students for doing what they are supposed to be doing?

ANSWER

For the same reason that adults like to pick up a paycheck. It is a way of letting me know I have done my job. If I do a really good job in the world of work, I might even get a raise. Students in the Fight-Free process are given audible praise for being fight free. How many of us work better when we get a compliment? Tangible rewards are just as effective with children and motivate them to reach incremental goals. In middle school programs, especially, principals find students motivated for things like a soda at lunch or a ticket to a ball game. Incentives in Fight Free for younger students are a button, ribbon, or sticker as a symbol of their accomplishment. Rewarding or noticing good deeds will ensure that good deeds continue.

Dr. Margaret R. Dolan

> *To prevent unwanted behavior, it is necessary to take a proactive, positive approach. Do we ever improve anyone by telling them how lousy they are? By appealing to the majority of students who are behaving appropriately and heralding their good citizenry, brings about the change in expectation from, "our school has problems" to, "we really do have a lot of students in this school who do know how to keep hands, feet, and all other objects to themselves."*

9. One teacher said that Fight Free worked because there was zero tolerance for fighting and it was enforced. If more principals just enforced a stern hand, then the incentives of Fight Free really do not work and would not be needed.

ANSWER

A firm hand has been used since the days of the hickory stick in the one-room school house. Some principals insist that they cannot use the "positive stuff" - "I have to use the hammer where I work." With violence in our schools on the rise, then it is clear to conclude that if we do what we have always done we will get the results we have always gotten. Relying on the code of conduct is a way to demonstrate our system of justice, much as we rely on our judicial system in society. To prevent unwanted behavior, it is necessary to take a proactive, positive approach. Do we ever improve anyone by telling them how lousy they are? By appealing to the majority of students who are behaving appropriately and heralding their good citizenry, brings about the change in expectation from, "our school has problems" to, "we really do have a lot of students in this school who do know how to keep hands, feet, and all other objects to themselves." Announcing that we have 530 students in our school and that 529 know how to keep hands, feet, and all other objects to themselves is much more appealing to the positive spirit of the school than saying, "We have one rotten apple in the whole bunch." Our bunch is not spoiled at all and tomorrow we will have 530 fight-free students.

10. Isn't it rather strict to say that any "hands-on" is a fight? After all, if a student just pushes another student, that is not a fight.

ANSWER

One day two students were waiting to see me outside my office. They were settling on the story they were going to tell me concerning their confrontation. They said, "Let's just tell her it was a push, not a fight. We were just playing around pushing so she won't tell us to take down the flag." Little did the perpetrators know that the evening before, I had watched the Lorana Bobbitt trial televised on cable television. The lawyer questioned Mr. Bobbitt, "Did you ever hit Lorana?" Mr. Bobbitt responded, "No, I never hit her, I just pushed her around a little." I rest my case.

11. What is the best way to set up the reward system?

ANSWER

The best way to set up the reward system is to have the planning team to brainstorm the things the students like to work for. What works at one school or with one age group might not work with another. Keep it simple, visible, and incremental. Emphasize school-wide, classroom and individual rewards, and be consistent.

School Violence...Calming the Storm

When planning with teachers, some principals have called and asked questions such as:

12. The classroom flag comes down when one person in that room didn't keep hands, feet, and all objects to themselves. What if the person from the classroom fought and the other person didn't fight. Is it fair that the other person who didn't fight still has to see the classroom flag come down?

ANSWER

The flag is a way of providing visual reinforcement of our success at rising to our expectations. If one person didn't keep hands, feet, and all other object to himself, then the classroom flag comes down. However, it can still be applauded that the school flag is still flying because the other person in the room didn't take the school flag down and still holds his/her individual Fight-Free pledge card or ribbon, button, etc. Keep it simple. Focus on the positive - all the students who didn't fight.

13. Teachers are confused about what a fight is.

ANSWER

A fight is two people exchanging aggressive physical contact. It can be a hit, a kick, a push, a bite, a thrown snowball, etc.

14. Kindergarten children have a tough time comprehending the message. Should they be involved?

ANSWER

Of course, kindergartners can have a tough time. At this stage developmentally, they are more impulsive, less likely to think first, then act. What helps is the daily role modeling of their kindergarten life situations: first in line problems, drinking fountain shoves, taking turns in a game, etc. Before starting them in Fight Free, dress rehearsal and dialogues that communicate what would happen if we were a Fight-Free School and we hit someone would be helpful. (See Primary Fight-Free Activity pages for reinforcements on courtesy and kindness to others.)

15. So, if I have a Fight-Free Plan in my school, will this ensure that I won't experience a tragedy like the one where two boys, ages 11 and 13, shot and killed several students and a teacher at a school in Jonesboro, Arkansas?

ANSWER

As a principal, when I read the headlines of the Jonesboro, Arkansas, incident, I paused and thought: That could be my school tomorrow and then I am thankful that it wasn't my school today. In the newspaper articles covering this incident, several students reported that the boys who had done the shooting said things like, "You will never see me again," and "There's going to be some killing here." **No program implemented can ensure that a school will not experience this kind of tragedy.** However, if we remember what our purpose in Fight Free is, it can help us by taking proactive measures to alert students to red flag statements such as, "There is going to be some killing here." One proactive measure that appears in one of the Fight-Free Front newsletters, is an anonymous hotline number. The number is posted in schools, ours is 839-SAFE and students can call anonymously, if they fear retribution, to

Dr. Margaret R. Dolan

report a gun, knife, drugs, or harassment. In our school district, our Director of Security worked with the local police agency to make this phone line possible. A working memorandum with your local police will help set up this system. Then, when school personnel talk about Code of Conduct or appropriate social skills, the hotline number can be referred to and the message of calling for help can be reinforced. We also publish this number in school newsletters. Another prevention to put in place is the Write-Not-Fight form. These forms, posted in classrooms and hallways, give students an opportunity to write down a concern and give it to school personnel. The more opportunities students have to talk about problems, the more able school staff become in being informed of potential red flag statements. Remember, such statements are cries for help.

16. If my school does not have a big problem with fighting, and we certainly do not have knives and guns, then why should we implement a Fight-Free Program?

ANSWER

One reason would be to celebrate the fact that you have so many students in your school who are meeting the expectations of "no fighting." Again, don't wait to have a problem. Prevention plans are the only remedy for the escalation of school violence across America. In a recent study entitled, "Violence and Discipline Problems in U.S. Public Schools," 100 percent of the serious violent crimes are in 10 percent of our schools. Some 90 percent of the 1,234 public schools surveyed had no incidents of serious violent crime in the school year 1996-97. This report only included incidents where the police were called to the school. So, as a principal, I may not call the police when one first grade student kicks another first grade student. However, to keep my school in the 90 percent that do not have incidents of serious violent crime, then a proactive approach would not leave it to chance. As the custodian of the safety of all students, I believe that a preventive plan would help keep the kicks from turning into assaults with knives or guns. Today, children have access to weapons to a greater degree than the students of thirty years ago. Building an awareness level of pro-social skills with students will hopefully lessen the chance that a student would choose to fight to solve a problem. One reason to implement the program would give you a forum to discuss appropriate behavior and celebrate the fact that your students are behaving in an acceptable manner.

The power is ours to determine our destination by the course of life that we follow, or to obscure it by the one that we fail to follow.

— Bertha Richardson
Classroom Teacher, Educational Consultant

CHAPTER 8
Fight Free Goes Preschool

When someone asked me how Fight Free would work in a middle school, my response was honest, "I don't know." However, my experience in education has led me to believe that some principles remain the same across age levels. We should all share the same goals for creating safe environments in our schools, however, we might attain the goal in different ways to serve the needs of our individual school communities. So, how would Fight Free work in a pre-school? Let's hear from Molly Dolan who decided to fly a Fight-Free Flag over her pre-school in Plano, Texas.

One weekend, this summer, I was in St. Louis to visit my family. While visiting with my Aunt Peggy, I talked with her about my five-year-old pre-school class. I told her all the cute things that the children did and how they loved creative movement and creative dramatics. I asked her if she could give me some advice. I told her how my children had a problem with hitting each other, kicking, throwing toys, and just fighting in general. I knew about the Fight-Free program, but I never thought to utilize the program in my pre-school room. Peggy brought out all of her literature and explained the program to me. She gave me a copy of her Write-Not-Fight form and some of the other articles about the Fight-Free Program.

I was very excited to get back to the pre-school and start Fight Free in my classroom. On the drive home from St. Louis to Dallas (where I live), I thought about how I could make Fight Free work. I finally came up with a plan. I started by getting a large Teddy bear that would be the KHFAAOOTY (Keep Hands, Feet, And, All Other, Objects To Yourself) Bear. I knew the Teddy bear would help the five-year-olds get excited about the Fight-Free Program. I also made my own version of the Fight-Free Flag. It had a pink background, a big Teddy bear on it, and the following quotes written in bright colors: KHFAAOOTY Bear says, "Keep Hands, Feet, and All Other Objects To Yourself." "Write-Not-Fight." "Miss Molly's class is Fight Free." I also made a bulletin board in my classroom that was the Fight-Free board. On it were index cards with a bear stamped on each card. Each card had a child's name on it from my class. Each child had an individual index card attached to the Fight-Free board when they came to

Dr. Margaret R. Dolan

school that Monday following my vacation. I also hung some Write-Not-Fight forms on the board which would be easy for my children to reach. As soon as all of the children arrived in the morning, we had circle time. All of the children and I sat in a circle on the carpet. I told them about our new Fight-Free Classroom. I told them that our neat, new flag was going to hang in our classroom. They became excited. I told them that the flag would be hanging if they had no fights in one day. I told them that a fight was when someone hit them and they hit, kicked, or pinched back. I told them that instead of fighting back, they could get a Write-Not-Fight form off the board, write the person's name down they were having trouble with, and give the form to me. (The children were able to copy names from name tags.) Then I would talk to both of them and we would try to work out the problem. I would tell the child who tried to start the fight that they could have used their words, called to the teacher, etc., instead of fighting.

I would then make the child who tried to fight take their name down from the Fight-Free board because they were not fight free for that day. I would thank the child who did not fight and tell them and the class that they kept the flag flying for the day. I also told the children what KHFAAOOTY meant and showed them the bear. We would all get to hold the bear on certain days if we could go a week without getting our names off the board. The kids also memorized the Fight-Free Motto, and if I asked them to say it and they could, they got to keep the bear with them for a while. The kids thought this was the coolest thing.

The other teachers in the pre-school thought it would never work. I thought that it couldn't hurt to try it because my kids had been fighting all the time. I also wrote a note home to the parents explaining the program. The parents loved the idea. Every day, when parents came to pick up their children, they would ask their child if his/her name had stayed on the board. The parents would make comments about the flag still flying. I could not believe the success of the program! The first week, I had about five children who had to take their names down. They were devastated, they cried, but they did not fight at all for the next few weeks.

After five months, I have only had to take the flag down once. The first time I took the flag down, the entire class started crying. The parents noticed the absence of the flag. The next morning, the children could not wait for that flag to go up. After the day the flag came down, I did not even get a Write-Not-Fight form for three weeks.

It is such an amazing program. The school day is so much easier and much more fun. I have noticed the kids stopping and thinking before they hit with blocks, feet, etc. I have also heard children saying that they didn't want the flag down and/or their names down, so that is why they have not fought. The parents are so pleased, as is the director of my school. I am so glad that my aunt gave me the idea. What a life-saver. It is so neat to watch these kids make good choices. I am so thankful for Fight Free.

Molly Dolan
Plano, Texas

As teachers, we provide a vital link to our most important natural resource, our youth. As educators, we are given the opportunity to daily support their basic needs and direct each student to identify the path to successful learning.

– Dee Blassie
*Classroom Teacher,
Educational Consultant*

Dr. Margaret R. Dolan

CHAPTER 9
The Carman Trails Elementary School Implementation Strategy

Having been a teacher of special education students for fifteen years, Peggy Dolan's FIGHT-FREE Program had a great deal of appeal for implementation into an entire school because of its ease of implementation and positive approach. I was able to chair the program for our elementary school, Carman Trails, and am continuing to do so with the approval of my principal, Mr. Robert Sainz. The incidents of altercation between students have been dramatically reduced in both physical and verbal reports. We celebrate weekly by wearing FIGHT-FREE hats on Fridays, classrooms have monthly awards for behavior, the school celebrates quarterly, and we even celebrate being FIGHT FREE the entire year. This program has made our school a more pleasant and non-threatening place to be, and we all love it!

Carol Littlefield
Classroom Teacher

Mission Statement

The mission of the FIGHT-FREE Schools Program is to teach the youth of today, the future leaders of our nation, appropriate interpersonal behavioral skills. The focus is to provide an improved school environment which will enhance the learning process and allow our children the optimum advantage to excel in their academic careers.

Students Rise to Fight-Free Expectations

What is a Fight-Free School?

- A school where the principal, staff, students, and parents set a goal to create a Fight-Free environment.

- A school where Fight-Free behavior is promoted, recognized and encouraged through daily praise, recognition, and role modeling.

- A school where Fight-Free behavior is discussed, taught, and practiced.

- A school where students become aware of alternative methods of dealing with anger and conflict.

Campaign Strategy Motivators

- Daily verbal praise recognizing Fight-Free behavior, public address system.

- Individual incentives for students stating "I'm a Fight-Free student," e.g., banners, ribbons, medals, trophies, caps, others.

- Classroom symbols of Fight-Free participations, e.g., banners, ribbons, medals, trophies.

- School-wide symbols, e.g., banners, flags, bumper stickers.

Dr. Margaret R. Dolan

Incorporating the 3 R's

RESPECT — Respect yourself, others and property. A willingness to show consideration, tolerance and good manners toward others and their property.

RESPONSIBILITY — A willingness to be accountable for your own actions.

RESTRAINT — A willingness to learn peaceful and acceptable methods of solving differences.

Motto: *Keep hands, feet, and all other objects to yourself.*

Definitions:

FIGHT: Two people are involved/infringing upon the rights of others by physically or verbally attacking another person.

HERO: Person who chooses to remain Fight Free and not respond to a physical or verbal altercation.

REPEAT OFFENDER: One who tries to interact with others in an inappropriate manner on a continuing basis. This might be manifested in a physical or verbal display of behavior.

REWARDS: Can be administered to individuals or groups of students who choose to remain Fight-Free. The rewards can be school-wide, involve grade levels, single classrooms, or may even be administered on an individual basis. The awards may be given by any person or persons.

School Violence...Calming the Storm

Rewards

These choices have been selected and effectively used:

Grade-level pizza parties

Extra recess time

Luncheons in the classroom

Popcorn parties

School-wide movies

Popsicles

Bowling parties

Skating parties

Coupons to spend at the school store

Arts/Crafts Classroom

Teacher-provided desserts for lunch

Repeat Offenders

COUNSELORS	will schedule time in the classrooms to speak with students about effective and acceptable ways of communicating which are approved by society.
CONFLICT MEDIATION	techniques will be used to help students learn to interact and deal with areas of conflict and disagreement.
INDIVIDUALS	will be selected to write a contract with the help of a classroom teacher or another person in the building. It might become necessary for students needing continued help to be seen on an individual basis by counselors. Classroom teachers might need to refer the students to the C.A.R.E. TEAM.

* FIGHT-FREE Implementation Plan developed by Carman Trails Elementary School, St. Louis, Missouri.

Dr. Margaret R. Dolan

Special Activity for the Repeat Offender

Objective

To address inappropriate behavior, engage in a contract to internalize appropriate behavior.

Procedure

- Have student write out what has been done.

- Use a Reflection Question form/Fight-Free Assessment (See Section V).

- If the student is a repeat offender, focus on why is it important to solve problems peacefully.

- With the student, design a contract to address the behavior. The intent is to begin to catalogue all of the times the student does not demonstrate the inappropriate behavior. The student will begin to reflect on more positive behavior and verbalize what he/she is thinking, feeling, and doing when his/her behavior is more appropriate.

- Develop a student chart. At intervals during the day, the teacher is able to look at the chart with the student and dialogue with him/her about the successful times.

Example:

Teacher: I noticed in music you had a plus. What did you do in music today? What were you thinking when you entered the class, during the class, at the end of the class? How did you feel when you achieved the plus (+)? In our next class, what will you do? If you are having a hard time, what can you do? What will you need to do to get a plus (+) for the next class?

The school counselor and teacher might discuss if the student would benefit from further interpersonal social skills activities with the counselor. A time limit should be put on the contract. Parents can be involved in the planning of the contract and offer verbal praise. Fixed celebrations or random celebrations are helpful in reinforcing the behavior. Being consistent about the reflection questions will lead toward intrinsic motivation to change behavior. If a student is successful in working off the contract system, then it is no longer required to continue its use. However, some students feel more comfortable with the parameters of the contract and respond positively over time to the structured focus on improved behavior.

Conclusion

The purpose of the contract is to improve the student's behavior. If behavior is improved then the student is able to join the fight-free ranks. If the student, after the time specified, improves behavior and chooses to continue to use the contract, he/she is still able to join the fight-free ranks again.

Dr. Margaret R. Dolan

Bibliography

Bernard, Cheryle. *Mediation Minus Morals.* Principal. Vol. 76, No. 2. 1996.

Boothe, James W.; Bradley, Leo; Flech, Michael T.; Keoug, Katherine K.; Kirk, Suzanne P. *The Violence at Your Door.* The Executive Educator. Vol. 15, No. 1. 1993.

Bryan, Bill; Autman, Samuel. *Shooting Injury Student.* St. Louis Post Dispatch. Nov. 1, 1996.

Cooperating School District. *Character Education Connection for School, Home and Community.* St. Louis, MO.

Crawford, Donna; Bodine, Richard. *Conflict Resolution Training: Peace Begins with Prevention.* National School Safety Center News Journal. Fall 1996.

Dolan, Margaret R. *Community Rises to Fight Free Expectations.* St. Louis Education Magazine, March/April 1994.

Faculty of the New City School. *Celebrating Multiple Intelligences: Teaching for success - A Practical Guide.* New City School. St. Louis, MO. 1994.

Ferguson Florissant School District. *Writer's Project.* Ferguson Florissant School District. Florissant, MO. May 1996.

Freiberg, H. Jerome. *From Tourist to Citizen in the Classroom.* Educational Leadership. Vol. 54, No. 1. Sept. 1996.

Gardner, Howard. *Frames of Mind: The Theory of Multiple Intelligences.* BasicBooks: NY. 1983.

Garritz, C.; Porte, W.; Sagen, N.; Short, Camilli, C. *Bully Proofing Your School: A Comprehension Approach.* National School Safety Center News Journal. Fall 1996.

Hodges, Ernest V.E.; Perry, David G. *Victimization is Never Just Child's Play.* National School Safety Center News Journal. Fall 1996.

Holsyter, Marlene C.; Sheldon, Don P. *Order Out of Chaos.* The Executive Educator. Vol. 16, No. 10. October 1994.

Jones, Rebecca. *Chaos Theory.* The Executive Educator. Vol. 16, No. 10. October 1994.

Latieri, Linda. *The Road to Peace in Our Schools.* Educational Leadership. Vol. 54, No.

1. September 1996.

Lewis, Catherine C; Schaps, Eric; Watson, Marilyn S. *The Caring Classroom Academic Edge.* Educational Leadership. Vol. 54, No. 1. September 1996.

Limber, Susan P. *Bullying Among School Children.* National School Safety Center News Journal. Fall 1996.

Mathematics Encyclopedia. *Math Puzzles, Graphs, Weights, Measures.* Rand McNally and Company. 1985.

Natale, JoAnna. *Your Life on the Line.* The Executive Educator. Vol. 16, No. 5. May 1994.

Ordonensky, Pat. *Facing Up To Violence.* The Executive Educator. Vol. 15, No. 1. 1993.

Schneider, Evelyn. *Giving Students a Voice in the Classroom.* Educational Leadership. Vol. 54, No. 1. September 1996.

Schwartz, Linzer. *Focus on the Learner.* Educational Psychology. Holbrook Press:Boston. 1997.

Smotherman, Jill. *Help for Victims and Bullies: Tease Out Success Potential.* National School Safety Center News Journal. Fall 1996.

Sousa, Chris; Peters, Carol; Peters, Mary. *Parents Become Advocates to Fight Disruption, Violence.* National School Safety Center News Journal. Fall 1996.

Thaler, Mike. *The Principal From the Black Lagoon.* Scholastic:NY.

U.S. Department of Education in partnership with the National Association of Elementary School Principals and the National Association of Secondary School Principals. *President's Education Awards Program.* www.naesp.org. peap@naesp.org.

Wasleben, Marjorie Creswell. *Bully Free Schools: What You Can Do.* National School Safety Center News Journal. Fall 1996.

World Book Encyclopedia. *Vol. N-O.* World Book, Inc. A Scott Fetzer Company. 1994.

World Book Encyclopedia. *Vol. WXYZ.* World Book, Inc. A Scott Fetzer Company. 1994.

Dr. Margaret R. Dolan

Wynn, Mychal; Blassie, Dee. *Building Dreams: Elementary School Teacher's Guide.* Rising Sun Publishing. Marietta, GA. 1995.

Wynn, Mychal. *The Change Continuum.* Rising Sun Publishing. Marietta, GA. 1998.

Wynn, Mychal. *The Eagles Who Thought They Were Chickens.* Rising Sun Publishing. Marietta, GA. 1994.

Wynn, Mychal. *The Eagles Who Thought They Were Chickens Student Activity Book.* Rising Sun Publishing. Marietta, GA. 1994.

Wynn, Mychal. *The Eagles Who Thought They Were Chickens Teacher's Guide.* Rising Sun Publishing. Marietta, GA. 1994.

Appendix

FIGHT FREE SCHOOLS

FIGHT-FREE ACTIVITIES OVERVIEW

The following activities support the entire concept of fight free. While the activities, as outlined are tried and proven, feel free to adapt them to your unique school situation. For example, the KHFAAOOTY Bear could become the KHFAAOOTY Dolphin, Eagle, etc., mascot for your school. For ease of implementation, we have included sample verbiage for each activity derived from hands-on implementation in the classroom and in school assemblies.

Activities Overview:

1. After the first successful year of the Fight-Free Program at McNair Elementary, Dr. Dolan promised the students that she would write an article to tell others what a great job the students had done in becoming fight free. This article might be used as a resource for staffs to read to become acquainted with the program. The article might also be shared with parents.

2. In the second year of the program, Dr. Dolan wanted to share the valuable effect that government and community involvement had on the success of the Fight-Free Program. This article was a useful resource for the school staff when planning for a Fight-Free Program. After reading the article, the planning team can chart what participation government leaders, business leaders, law enforcement officers, and others will have in the implementation of the Fight-Free Program.

3. Sample newspaper articles are included to provide samples of how other schools implement the Fight-Free Program. A variety of ideas will help to generate discussion about which ideas will work for individual buildings. Schools are encouraged to call the local news media so that the students receive coverage for their Fight-Free efforts.

4. The Fight-Free Ticket-To-Peace is an extension of the Fight-Free Program and can be used to involve government, law enforcement officers and parents. (See the sample Ticket-To-Peace.) Each school is invited to ask their local mayor, chief of police, D.A.R.E. Officer or other local leaders to add a quote for the school's Ticket-To-Peace brochure. The Ticket-To-Peace is another way for children to communicate confrontational situations on the way to school or on the way home from school and can empower students with the ability to solve problems in a peaceful manner and to seek appropriate assistance in doing so.

5. A Fight-Free Check List will help the planning team verify that they have all necessary components to ensure the success of the program when implemented.

6. When the Fight-Free Program began, it's application to middle schools and high schools was questioned. A middle school researched the elementary program and designed the incentives to better suit middle school students. Included in this section are samples of middle school implementations. Planning teams might get some ideas that would be suitable for implementing the Fight-Free Program in their schools.

7. Fight-Free Newsletters are published to provide a forum for sharing ideas from other schools. Newsletters are included to broaden the fight-free picture for planning teams and can serve as resource material when introducing the program to others.

8. Write-Not-Fight forms are effective tools for students to communicate, in writing, that they are experiencing confrontational situations. Provided is a sample to use for primary students in case they are not fluent in writing skills, and a sample for intermediate. Middle Schools have used the Ticket-To-Peace brochure for their students. Forms are placed on teachers' desks, at doorways and at locations where students congregate. Forms are available and help to signal to the teacher, counselor, or principal that there is a problem and that someone needs assistance. Schools using peer mediation find the forms useful in setting up peace talks.

9. Fight-Free Bus Baseball. School buses are counted separate from the In-School Fight-Free events. Bus Baseball is a way to keep score. Each bus starts off with the Official Fight-Free Bus Score Sheet. Bus drivers place bus numbers and can keep score on this sheet. The baseball diamond is posted in the front of the bus. If students on the bus have no bus write-ups for a week, then they fill in first base. After the second week of no bus write-ups, they fill in second base. They continue until they reach home plate. At lunchtime, they receive 5 points. Five points earns them the bronze division certificate and a new baseball diamond is posted. When 10 points are achieved, they reach the silver division. When 15 points are achieved, they receive the Gold division certificate. Your school newsletter or district paper might record the status of the buses at your school. Announcements on the public address system are quick and easy ways to celebrate students' fight-free status.

10. The Fight-Free Families Pages can be sent home and parents can follow suggestions to help their children solve sibling family squabbles. The letter can be personalized for your school and the pages can be duplicated and folded to create a pamphlet.

Dr. Margaret R. Dolan

Section I
Planning

"Coming Together is a Beginning"

Form a Fight Free School Team: The mission of this team will be to plan the Fight Free implementation strategy unique to your school community. On your planning team, invite staff representatives, students, parents, community leaders, business partners and law enforcement personnel. When selecting your team, remember:

"As a rule of thumb, involve everyone in everything."
– Tom Peters

- Before the team meets, provide each person with the selected resource material to read.

- When the team meets, pose the question: "How will the Fight-Free process work in our school to make (your school name) Fight Free?

- Review the Fight-Free Mission Statement and adapt as necessary to your school.

- Agree on definitions.

- Agree on Code of Conduct.

- Agree on process to inform staff, students, and parents.

- Agree on trial run time line.

- Agree on procedures for individual, classroom and school-wide plan.

- Agree on kick-off date and kick-off assembly.

- Agree on evaluation check points.

- Agree on PTA/PTO participation.

- Agree on community leaders participation.

- Agree on business participation.

- Agree on law enforcement personnel involvement.

Dr. Margaret R. Dolan

"Keeping Together is Progress"
Fight-Free Planning Paradigm

Assignment	Team Members	Resources Required	Responsibilities	Due Date	Evaluation Process/Date
Fight-Free Planning Team					
Staff Development					
Parent Development					
Code of Conduct					
Definition/ Procedures					
Business Involvement					
Community Leaders Involved					
On-Going Student Ed. Plan					
Kick-off Assemblies					
Advertising Plan					
Incentives					
Classroom					
Individual					
School-wide					

"Working Together is Success"

School Violence...Calming the Storm

Section II
Behavior Workshop

The Behavior Workshop will provide the following:

- Information on the brain.

- Information on emotions and learning.

- Strategies to use when confronted with conflict.

- Role playing fight-free behavior.

- Appropriate interpersonal social skills to use in creating a fight-free school climate.

Dr. Margaret R. Dolan

The Brain and Fight Free

Materials

- Overhead of the brain labeled with Neocortex and Limbic System.
- "Control Your Anger" poster.

Procedure

- *The teacher will say to the class,* "Raise your hand if you ever heard mom, dad, or grandpa say, 'Count to ten so you don't get mad. Count to ten and you will calm down and not blow up.' Did you ever wonder why they said that? What we're going to find out today is how our brain can keep us fight free. Here's a model of how the parts of our brain work." *Point to and have students read the words as you point.* "Can you think of some times in school when you use the Neocortex?" *Invite responses.*

Conclusion

- "For us to be successful in spelling, math, reading, science, and social studies, we need to keep the Neocortex working."

- "Now let's read what the Limbic System is all about. Notice where the Limbic System is in relation to the thinking or cognitive part. Can I use a student's head for a profile?" Use a student from the group. "Let's see, the Neocortex is up here *(point to top of student's head)* and the Limbic is here *(point to back of student's head near neck area)*. If someone is frightened or angered, what portion of the brain is being used? The Limbic." *Point to neck area.*

- "And what happens when our adrenaline pumps and the blood flow gets started? If you don't stop and think, the immediate response, when angered, is to attack. That's why people have attack dogs. Dogs don't think, they attack. Since we have a part of the brain that dogs don't, we can count to 10, giving our blood time to travel up to the Neocortex (point to student's head and overhead). We can visualize not fighting, what to do instead of attacking, so we can think our way out. Some of you might recall the 'Control Your Anger' poster. Who would like to read some things to do when angry?"

School Violence...Calming the Storm

The Human Brain

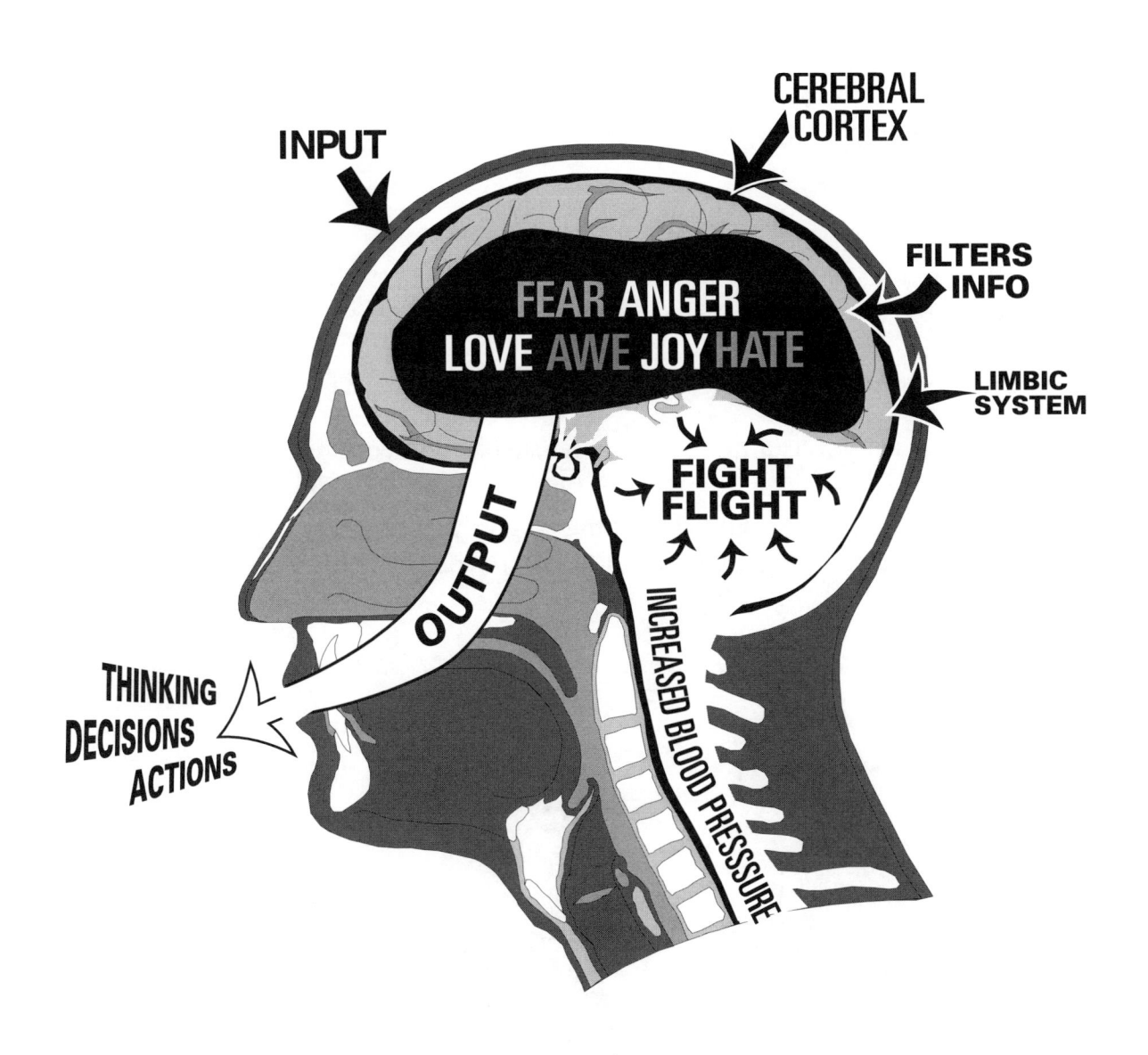

Dr. Margaret R. Dolan

Role Playing

"Now let's think of some ways we can help ourselves out of some real problems at school. Sometimes students get sent to the office for things like:

- hitting
- kicking
- pushing and
- destroying property.

Let's take a look at what you can do if you are hassled by someone so that you don't fight. Can you tell me what a fight is? A fight is when two people exchange aggressive blows. It takes two to fight. I'm going to give you some 'I' statements you can use to give you time to stop and think and maybe you'll help the other person to stop and think."

(Have two students prepared with role playing problems and "I" statements.)

Role Playing, continued

Problem 1: One student calls another a name.

Student A: "You are ugly."

Student B: "I don't like what you said."

"I feel badly because you hurt my feelings."

"I don't want you to do it again."

Student A: "You are double ugly."

Student B: "I will count to 10."

"I will use a Write-Not-Fight form."

"I will get help."

What would happen if Student B got mad and called Student A a name?

Problem 2: One student pushes another student.

Student A: Butts in line and pushes Student B.

Student B: "I don't like what you did."

"I feel badly because you hurt me."

"I don't want you to do it again."

"I will get help."

What would happen if Student B pushed Student A back?

Role play can occur in a line in the restroom, playing outside on the playground, arguing over "safe" or "out" in baseball games, a problem on the bus, e.g., someone spit on another, etc.

"Now let's fill in our posters." (Invite students to fill in the posters)

Dr. Margaret R. Dolan

Playground

What do students do on a Fight-Free Playground:

Look Like:	Sound Like:	Feel Like:
Take turns	Listen	Happy
Polite behavior	"Excuse me."	Exciting
No pushing	Laugh	Joyful
No tagging	Loud voices	Safe

School Violence...Calming the Storm

Cafeteria

What do students do in a Fight-Free Cafeteria:

Look Like:	Sound Like:	Feel Like:
Orderly	6" voices	Content
Polite behavior	No yelling	Safe
Obey rules	No bad words	Happy
Cooperative	Polite words	Pats on back

Dr. Margaret R. Dolan

Restroom

What do students do in a Fight-Free Restroom:

Look Like:	Sound Like:	Feel Like:
Clean	6" voices	Safe
No graffiti	No yelling	Calm
Orderly	No name-calling	Courteous

Bus

What do students do on a Fight-Free Bus:

Look Like:	Sound Like:	Feel Like:
In seats	1" voices	Safe
Orderly	No name-calling	Good
Calm	Respectful	Happy

Dr. Margaret R. Dolan

Line

What do students in a Fight-Free line:

Look Like:	Sound Like:	Feel Like:
Organized	Quiet	Responsible
Respectful	Polite	Reliable
Straight	Good listeners	Pleased

School Violence...Calming the Storm

Section III
KHFAAOOTY Bear Activities

Dr. Margaret R. Dolan

KHFAAOOTY
by Betty Seibert
McNair Reading Specialist

Khfaaooty is an acronym for: **Keep Hands, Feet, And All Other Objects To Yourself.**

Khfaaooty has become the personification of our number one rule. He is a lovable bear that is regularly enrolled in all school activities. He wears a McNair Fight-Free T-shirt on most days as he sits in the office to welcome new students and visitors.

Khfaaooty's outfit may change as he participates in other school activities. During standardized testing week, Khfaaooty sat in a student desk in the front hall reminding students and visitors to be especially quiet in the halls and to do their best. Each testing day, a rhyme with a message of encouragement was received by each student from Khfaaooty.

Khfaaooty also participated in "Read Across America" wearing a Dr. Seuss hat and holding a bag of books. Students sat in rocking chairs next to Khfaaooty and took turns rocking and reading.

Older students enjoyed having the bear visit the classroom, but were less likely to hold him. He was useful, however, to them as they explained behavioral expectations to younger students. The students in the upper grades were expected to both explain and model appropriate "Khfaaooty" behavior for younger students. This attitude promoted the family feeling of shared responsibility, but also gave older students experience in putting into words and practice the non-violent values we have been trying to instill in them. The hope is that the ability to articulate the reasons for non-violent behavior will help them in middle school. Other programs such as D.A.R.E. and PEER POWER combined with FIGHT FREE will help to make our students leaders and less susceptible to negative peer pressure.

In addition to welcoming new students, encouraging good effort on tests, and participating in special events, Khfaaooty is a continuous reminder to **Keep Hands, Feet, And All Other Objects To Yourself.**

School Violence...Calming the Storm

Keep Hands, Feet, And All Other Objects To Yourself

My Name: _____

Write-Not-Fight

I am having a problem. Please help.

Thank you,

Keep Hands, Feet, And All Other Objects To Yourself

My Name: _____

Write-Not-Fight

I am having a problem. Please help.

Thank you,

Primary

Dr. Margaret R. Dolan

Keep Hands, Feet, And All Other Objects To Yourself

Name: _____ Grade: _____

I am having a problem with: _____

Who: _____

Where: _____

When: _____

I have tried these things: _____

_____

_____

I am upset because: _____

_____

_____

To solve the problem I am going to: _____

_____

_____

Intermediate

Hugging: *The perfect cure for whatever ails you.*

No moving parts
No batteries to wear out
No periodic checkups
Low-energy consumption
High-energy yield
Inflation proof
No monthly payments
No insurance requirements
Theft proof
Non-taxable
Non-polluting
And, of course, fully returnable
Hugging is healthy
Relieves tension
Combats depression
Reduces stress
Improves blood circulation
Is invigorating
Is rejuvenating
Elevates self-esteem
Has no unpleasant side effects
Is nothing less than a miracle drug

– Florida Teddy Bear

Dr. Margaret R. Dolan

Fight-Free Mascot

The KHFAAOOTY Bear

You can color KHFAAOOTY Bear and fill in the word bubbles.

Can you guess what KHFAAOOTY stands for?

_____ _____ _____ _____ _____

_____ _____ _____ _____

Primary

School Violence...Calming the Storm

KHFAAOOTY Bear Pledge Card

Our rule is: Keep Hands, Feet, And All Other Objects To Yourself.

KHFAAOOTY Bear:

KHFAAOOTY is here to help us remember our rule. I'll have all of the fight-free names of students in a hat. Each day, I'll pick out a fight-free student who can take KHFAAOOTY to class." *Select a student.*

After doing this for several weeks, some sixth grade boys asked if the Student Government could buy smaller stuffed bears, call them KHFAAOOTY Juniors and give one to each homeroom so that more students could hold KHFAAOOTY. Sixth graders, too, take advantage of the the creativity that comes from students.

Pledge Card:

Each student receives a pledge card to sign as a member of fight free. Students who are sent to the office for not being Fight Free will bring their pledge cards to the office not to be returned until they have served their consequences.

Fight-Free Pledge

I promise to do my best to be Fight Free.

To respect myself and others in word and deed and to keep my hands, feet, and all other objects to myself.

By being Fight Free, I will help our school be the best it can be for you and me.

Together we will be Fight Free!

All Levels

Dr. Margaret R. Dolan

KHFAAOOTY Talk

Objective

To create dialogue/role playing to develop "I" statements.

Materials

- A stuffed bear or a cut-out paper bear.
- Craft paper cut into word bubbles.

Procedure

- *The teacher introduces KHFAAOOTY.*

- *Write large letters on the board and ask students to say the one Fight-Free rule: "Keep Hands, Feet, And All Other Objects To Yourself."*

- *Invite students to discover what the name KHFAAOOTY (affectionately pronounced KHFAAOOTY) means.*

- *After discovering what the word represents, explain that KHFAAOOTY is going to help us learn ways that we can talk to each other in a peaceful way and help us remember to be Fight Free.*

- *Ask the students if they remember the "I" statements from the behavior workshop.*

Primary

List them on the chalkboard in the bubbles.

- "I don't like what you said/did."
- "I feel badly because you hurt me/hurt my feelings."
- "I don't want you to do it again."
- "I will count to 10."
- "I will use a Write-Not-Fight form."
- "I will get help."

Role Playing: *Have one student at a time hold KHFAAOOTY. Read the problem and have the student choose the appropriate word bubble.*

Problem:

- Someone called you a name.
- Someone butted in line.
- Someone took your food from the lunch tray.
- Someone made a face at you.
- Someone hit you.
- Someone took your seat on the bus

"I don't want you to do it again."

"I will get help."

"I will use a Write-Not-Fight form."

"I feel bad because you hurt me/hurt my feelings."

"I don't like what you said/did."

"I will count to 10."

Dr. Margaret R. Dolan

KHFAAOOTY Planner

Objectives

- To encourage students to keep track of their KHFAAOOTY behavior.
- To teach students the days of the week.
- To teach students organizational skills.

Materials

- KHFAAOOTY stickers.
- KHFAAOOTY planner page.
- Fight-Free Assessment Sheet.

Procedure

- Students will add the KHFAAOOTY planner page to their Fight-Free Journals. Students will use their Fight-Free Assessment Sheets to decide if they should receive a KHFAAOOTY sticker. The teacher will guide those who experience difficulty through their assessments. Teachers and students will discuss the decisions. Teachers will read the assessments aloud.

Note: Utilize the following pages by writing in the dates for each month. Each month can be used by individual teachers to communicate testing days, special events, and other classroom information to parents. They can also be used by the school administration for communicating the fight-free process throughout the school year.

The KHFAAOOTY illustrations and captions can also be cut and pasted onto other flyers that are sent home to parents to keep everyone focused on fight-free behavior.

School Violence...Calming the Storm

	Monday	Tuesday	Wednesday	Thursday	Friday
Week 1					
Week 2					
Week 3					
Week 4					
Week 5					

Things to Remember When You Become Angry

1. Remove yourself from the situation. Count to 10 and calm down.

2. Tell an adult what made you angry.

3. Write out your problem.

4. Plan ways to make peace.

5. Seek help from someone–a teacher or a parent.

6. Be honest. By telling the truth, you will be telling what your role in the situation was.

7. Name-calling, arguing, and physically fighting will make the situation worse.

8. To solve a problem, communicate clearly and appropriately.

Section IV
Classroom Activities

Dr. Margaret R. Dolan

Fight-Free Crest

The Fight-Free Schools' Crest

Using the Fight-Free Schools' Crest enables a school to involve students in creating its own designs to be added to the crest. The following is an explanation of the crest and how to symbolize it for an individual school.

- The dividing lines of the crest represent the Peace Symbol.

- The book in section three of the crest represents academic achievement through learning, which is a school's ultimate goal.

- In sections one and two, school's may add a variety of symbols that represent their individual schools. Suggestions include the school's mascot or slogan, the school colors, or other symbols created by students to represent school spirit.

School Violence...Calming the Storm

Fight-Free Self-Assessment

Objective

To allow students to assess their own behavior.

Materials

- Pencil
- Assessment sheet
- Fight-Free Bulletin Board "Control Your Anger" poster.

Procedure

- *The teacher will read each assessment statement to students and invite them to respond with a <u>Yes</u> or <u>No</u>.*
- *Refer to the "Control Your Anger" poster and review. Conference individually with students allowing them to verbalize how they responded, giving examples.*
- *This sheet is effective with students who have had a discipline referral with a teacher, principal, or counselor.*

Primary

Dr. Margaret R. Dolan

Fight-Free Self-Assessment

1. I was Fight Free today.

   _____

   _____

2. I solved a problem or problems peacefully.

   _____

   _____

3. I used one of the steps from our "Controlling Your Anger" poster.

   _____

   _____

4. I shared my problem with someone who could help me.

   _____

   _____

5. I told the truth.

   _____

   _____

6. Tomorrow I will be Fight Free.

   _____

   _____

Primary

Fight-Free Journal

Objective

To create a personal Fight-Free Journal design as a cover for collecting fight-free activities, writings, quotes, pictures, thoughts, etc.

Materials

A spiral notebook or loose-leaf papers and card stock for cover, art supplies, markers, pencils.

Procedure

Have students use a spiral notebook or direct them to assemble loose-leaf papers and card stock to make a notebook.

- *At the chalkboard, invite students to brainstorm different ideas which they could include when thinking about designing a personal cover for their Fight-Free Journals.*

- *Discuss a variety of activities that could be included, e.g., fight-free quotes from famous people, fight-free activities from classroom participation, fight-free cheers, songs, slogans, fight-free problem-solving dialogue.*

- **Benefits of the journal:** When a student has a problem, the teacher and student are able to use the journal to initiate a dialogue about alternatives to violence. Future fight-free activities are included in the fight-free Journal, e.g., use the Fight-Free Assessment Activity (see Activity). Even a student not having a problem may review it as a reinforcement for their behavior.

Primary/Intermediate

Dr. Margaret R. Dolan

Fight-Free Bulletin Board

Objective

To contribute to the creation of a Fight-Free Bulletin Board in the classroom.

Materials

Bulletin board items, letters, art supplies.

Procedure

Designate a bulletin board in your room to be the Fight-Free Bulletin Board.

- *Students can make decisions about permanent and changeable items.*

- *Permanent items might include: Fight-Free Pledge Card, flag, anger poster.*

- *Changeable items that students could be responsible for updating might include: Number of days the Fight-Free Flag is up, classroom fight-free days, school-wide fight-free days, fight-free writings, quotes, songs, cheers, and KHFAAOOTY says bubbles.*

Primary/Intermediate

Fight-Free Peaceful Words

Objective

To share previous knowledge of the word/concept **peace** through discussions.

Materials

Chalkboard or overhead, poster board, markers.

Procedure

- *List synonyms and antonyms for the word peace and for other words such as: respect, integrity, cooperation. Post around the room or as an addition to the Fight-Free Bulletin Board.*

- *Write the word peace on the chalkboard, overhead transparency, or poster board. Using poster board, the results can be displayed for reference in future fight-free activities.*

- *Ask discussion questions like:*

  What do you think of when you hear the word **peace**?

  What pictures come to your mind when you hear the word **peace**?

  In pairs, brainstorm all of the synonyms for **peace** you can think of. *Allow one minute.*

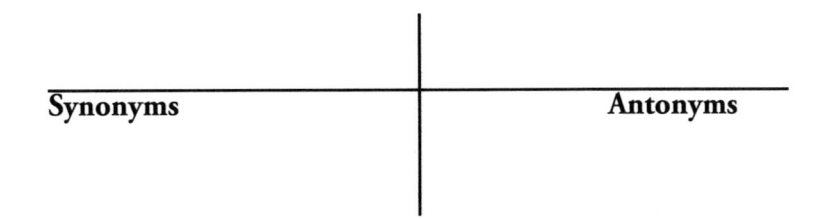

Synonyms	Antonyms

- Pair shared responses and record on class chart. Display for future activities.

Primary/Intermediate

Dr. Margaret R. Dolan

Fight-Free Peace and Careers

Objective

To brainstorm for generating a list of careers.

Procedure

- *Begin lesson by having students share their ideas on how a career is different from a job.*

- *Draw a conclusion with class input about what a career is.*

- *Have students brainstorm list of careers.*

- *Students may research the careers of their choice through texts or interviews of persons in that career.*

- *Role play dialogues with persons in careers where a conflict has occurred.*

    What would a dialogue with a co-worker look like?

    What would a dialogue with a customer/patient/client sound like?

- "Think about the person in the career you have chosen. What words would describe the way a peaceful person would act?"

Primary/Intermediate

Fight-Free T-Shirt

Objective

To design and create a personal Fight-Free T-Shirt.

Materials

T-shirt. (For the purpose of a permanent display, students can cut a t-shirt from craft paper to hang on a line in the classroom.)

Procedure

- *Lead the students in a discussion of Fight Free. A secretary will take notes at the board listing students' ideas. Students will share their knowledge of Fight Free, i.e., Flag, Write-Not-Fight forms, Behavior Workshop, Pledge, etc.*

- "Design and create your own personal Fight-Free T-Shirts."

Dr. Margaret R. Dolan

Fight-Free Flag

Objective

To design a Fight-Free Flag.

Materials

- Poster board

- Art supplies

- Fight-Free Flag explanation (how to make a Fight-Free Flag; see additional resources section).

Procedures

- *Share the Fight-Free School Crest with students and discuss the components.*

- *Discuss what a Peace Symbol is. Ask if anyone knows the history of the Peace Symbol and how it came to be.* (A trip to the library or Internet would assist in the research.)

- *Invite students to create their own Fight-Free Flag.* (Some schools have a contest to decide the school flag.)

School Violence...Calming the Storm

Fight-Free Song

Objective

To compose a Fight-Free Song.

Materials

Samples of songs written by students with the fight-free message and the Fight-Free Journal.

Procedures

- *Students will participate in singing songs that have the fight-free message. Explain that students from other fight-free schools wrote lyrics to tunes they already knew.*

- *Students can do the same with fight-free cheers also, e.g.,:*

  "Give me an: F   F
                I   R
                G   E
                H   E
                T

  What does it spell?

  Can't hear you!

  Louder!!!"

Dr. Margaret R. Dolan

Fight-Free Self-Assessment Reflection Questions

Objective

To engage in an intrapersonal and interpersonal activity for reflecting and responding after a confrontation has occurred.

Procedures

- Students might use this for role playing in pairs or small groups.

- Reflection questions should be used with individuals who have been part of a conflict. Judge Judy terms for the students who should participate in the reflection question activity should be the "perpetrator" and the "victim." At times, when two students are in a conflict, it is a challenge to determine who the perpetrator is because as students tell their version, with no interruptions from the other person. When both sides have shared, ask students the reflection questions. Upper grade students might write answers in their Fight-Free Journals. Younger students might write answers in their Fight-Free Journals. Younger students could respond verbally. This is effective to use for name-calling.

- Another tool to use at times where actual hands-on, aggressive behavior occurs would be the Fight-Free Assessment form. Allowing the students time to reflect on what they have done affords an opportunity for the reinforcement of the lessons involved in the Fight-Free Workshop and in their Fight-Free Journals.

Intermediate

Fight-Free Self-Assessment

Place a check ✓ next to the fight-free tips you have followed:

1. ❑   I practiced the Fight-Free Pledge.

2. ❑   I used fight-free language.

3. ❑   I used one of the ideas from the "Control Your Anger" poster.

4. ❑   I have set a good example by keeping hands, feet, and all other objects to myself.

5. ❑   I will be Fight Free tomorrow.

Intermediate

Dr. Margaret R. Dolan

Reflection Questions

1. What were you thinking when...

2. How did it make you feel?

3. What would you say if someone did that to you?

4. How would you feel if someone did that to you?

5. What will you do if you become angry at someone the next time?

6. What will you do if someone hurts you or hurts your feelings?

7. How do you think the other person felt?

8. What can you say to let the other person know how you feel?

9. Why is it important to solve problems peacefully at school?

10. How will learning to solve problems peacefully now help you in the future?

Intermediate

What it means to me to be in a Fight-Free School

F
I
G
H
T

F
R
E
E

S
T
U
D
E
N
T

Intermediate

Dr. Margaret R. Dolan

Fight-Free Box

Objective

To contribute ideas and create items to be included in the Fight-Free Box.

Materials

Shoe box, gift box, grocery box, art supplies.

Procedure

Introduce lesson by inviting students to share how they would feel if they suddenly had to go to a new school.

- *After discussion, invite students to share the ways we help new students.*

- *After sharing, invite students to think of a way to help new students in our classroom learn about Fight Free.*

- *Brainstorm what they need to know. After brainstorming, lead students to categorize their list. Divide students into cooperative learning groups and assign each group the task of deciding how the group can best represent their categories by contributing an item in the book, i.e., a sample Fight-Free Journal, a sample Fight-Free School Flag, classroom flag or individual incentive. Students must have a set of directions or an explanation attached to the items.*

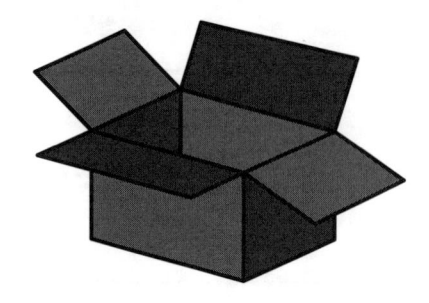

Primary/Intermediate

Solving Problems

Objective

To use a cartoon medium to apply fight-free strategies in solving problems peacefully.

Materials

- Newspaper comics
- Art paper
- Art supplies

Procedures

- *Students can choose from newspaper or comic book cartoons examples of the fight-free message.*

- *Using the cartoon characters, students will create a fight-free cartoon. The cartoon characters will use strategies from the "Control Your Anger" Poster or those presented in the Behavior Workshop.*

- *Students might choose cartoon characters with children involved, e.g.,* **Family Circus, Dennis the Menace, Charlie Brown.**

Intermediate

Dr. Margaret R. Dolan

Verbal/Linguistic

Logical/Mathematical

Visual/Spatial

Bodily/Kinesthetic

Section V
Multiple Intelligences Activities

Interpersonal

Intrapersonal

Musical/Rhythmic

Naturalist

EXCERPT FROM:
THE CHANGE CONTINUUM
BY MYCHAL WYNN

The theory of Multiple Intelligences provides an effective approach for developing implementation strategies pertaining to the components of school change. By developing an implementation strategy pertinent to each of the eight areas of intelligence identified by Howard Gardner (seven of which are outlined in the book, *Frames of Mind*) we create a multi-faceted instructional approach to solutioning the unique needs of our school community.

While we may still lack substantive research regarding Multiple Intelligences application to the process of school change I personally have witnessed the synergy and effectiveness of this approach. My experience with Multiple Intelligences grouping is a practical application of the adage "Great minds think alike." Those highly developed in Logical/Mathematical Intelligence effortlessly arrive at a series of practical steps toward effecting change. Likewise, those highly developed in Visual/Spatial Intelligence effortlessly identify visually stimulating components which seemed to transform the school culture and climate. It follows that those highly developed in Verbal/Linguistic, Interpersonal, and Intrapersonal conceptualize the language, sprit of teamwork, and goals that nurture and in many cases provide the catalyst for change. The Body/Kinesthetic, Musical/Rhythmic, and Naturalist Intelligences forge the overall spirit of change through sound, movement, and the environment.

Think of it, the person who relies upon Logical/Mathematical Intelligence may never "see" the importance of a visually stimulating and inspiring environment as seen through the unique processing abilities of those highly developed in Visual/Spatial Intelligence. Yet, does one outweigh the importance of the other in fostering a nurturing school culture and climate?

Dr. Margaret R. Dolan

Verbal/Linguistic Intelligence

The ability to think in words. Responsible for the production of language and all the complex possibilities that follow, including: poetry, humor, story-telling, abstract reasoning, and the written word.

Logical/Mathematical Intelligence

The ability to calculate, quantify, and carry out complex mathematical operations. Associated with what is called "scientific thinking." Deductive/inductive thinking/reasoning, numbers and recognition of abstract patterns.

Interpersonal Intelligence

Ability to understand others and their feelings. Ability to work cooperatively in a group as well as the ability to communicate, verbally and non-verbally with other people.

Intrapersonal Intelligence

Knowledge of the internal aspects of self including the ability to plan and direct one's life. Ability to understand such areas as inner feelings, spirituality, range of emotional responses, self-reflection, and sense of intuition.

Visual/Spatial Intelligence

The capacity to think in three-dimensional terms. Ability to create internal mental pictures. Deals with such things as the visual arts, navigation, map-making, and architecture.

Musical/Rhythmic Intelligence

Sensitivity to pitch, melody, and rhythm including such capacities as the recognition and use of rhythmic and tonal patterns, sensitivity to sounds such as the human voice and musical instruments.

Body/Kinesthetic Intelligence

The ability to manipulate objects and fine-tune physical skills. Ability to use the body to express emotion as in dance, karate, gymnastics, body language, and sports. The ability to learn by doing.

Naturalist Intelligence

The ability to recognize plants, animals, and other parts of the natural environment, like clouds or rocks.

KHFAAOOTY

Objective

To engage in a fight-free activity using Verbal/Linguistic; Logical/Mathematical; Visual/Spatial; Interpersonal; Intrapersonal; Bodily/Kinesthetic; and Musical/Rhythmic Intelligences.

Materials

- KHFAAOOTY Bear
- List of Multiple Intelligences Attachments
- KHFAAOOTY Poem
- Samples of Fight-Free Songs, and Cheers

Procedures

- "We are all smart in many ways. With our brains, we can dance, sing, write, play sports, etc." *Write the list on the board.*
- *Review list on the board and invite students to give examples of what KHFAAOOTY would be doing if he was exercising that intelligence.*

Hi, I'm KHFAAOOTY Bear and I know all of my intelligences!

Dr. Margaret R. Dolan

Multiple Intelligences Activities with KHFAAOOTY

Intelligence	Fight-Free Class Activity	Individual/Group Activity
Verbal/Linguistic	Recite the KHFAAOOTY Talk Poem (see poem).	Create your own Fight-Free Poem.
Logical/Mathematical	Make a graph of the school's fight-free days.	Keep a graph/chart in your Journal of your fight-free days.
Visual/Spatial	Color/draw KHFAAOOTY in a line at school.	Design a personal Fight-Free Flag.
Musical/Rhythmic	Sing the Fight-Free Song (see sample).	Create words to a Fight-Free Song.
Bodily/Kinesthetic	Create actions to go with a Fight-Free Cheer ("Give me a F-I-G-H-T").	Create your own Fight-Free Cheer.
Intrapersonal	Discuss/write how you feel when you see the Fight-Free Flag flying. How would you feel if we had to take it down?	Write in your Journal or draw a picture of how you feel when you see the Fight-Free Flag flying.
Interpersonal	Role play fight-free behavior.	Write dialogue for a Write-Not-Fight form.

School Violence...Calming the Storm

KHFAAOOTY Talk Poem

KHFAAOOTY says: *When playing games use KHFAAOOTY words. Here's a KHFAAOOTY poem. Listen and circle the KHFAAOOTY words you hear. Can you circle KHFAAOOTY words?*

KHFAAOOTY Poem

When asking for something,
remember it's polite to say, "Please."
other words to say are, "Thank you,"
for something you receive.

If someone's feelings are hurt,
and they are feeling bad,
saying, I'm sorry, will help them
not feel sad.

If you're in the hall,
and you get bumped
and bump the next person in line,
say, "Excuse me!"
and everything will be fine.

When you see someone,
*Keep Hands, Feet, And All Other Objects
To Yourself.*
Say, "Good job!" or "Way to go!"
To show you're glad they're doing well.

Dr. Margaret R. Dolan

Nobel Peace Prize

Objectives

To research information about the Nobel Peace Prize.

To select a Nobel Peace Prize winner and research his/her life.

To create a poster displaying research findings.

Materials

- A visit to the library or Internet
- Poster board
- Art supplies

Procedures

- *Discuss with students the awards they know of where people have received commendation for something, e.g., Academy Award, Pulitzer Prize, Heismann Trophy.*
- *Introduce a prize for Peace as the Nobel Peace Prize.*
- *Students will be invited to research what the award is and how one is nominated and receives the award.*
- *Students are then invited to choose a person who has been awarded the Nobel Prize for Peace.*
- *After researching, the student will create a poster either individually, in pairs, or in cooperative learning groups to represent the person. An oral presentation will unveil the poster.*
- *Present participants with Nobel Peace Prize Certificates for their efforts.*

Intermediate

Interview Questions

Interview parents and others on the importance of <u>peace</u> in their careers.

1. How are problems solved where you work?
   _____
   _____
   _____

2. If a person at your place of work has a problem with another person, how do they go about solving it **peacefully**?
   _____
   _____
   _____

3. What examples of **peace** do you see at your place of work?
   _____
   _____

4. Can you think of a time when you helped bring **peace** at your job?
   _____
   _____
   _____

Discussion Questions:

- How are your examples like the examples on our anger poster?
- Did anyone share an example that was different from what we do at school to solve problems?
- From the interviews, make a list of the variety of the types of work.
- Does the type of work done require a different method for solving problems peacefully?

Primary/Intermediate

Dr. Margaret R. Dolan

Discussion Questions, continued

Lead the students to conclude that in every career, although the type of work is different, the methods for problem solving, peacefully, are the same.

- "Choose a career in which you are interested."
- "Create a problem on the job."
- "Tell the ways you would problem solve. Include the dialogue you would use in your essay."

Multiple Intelligences Careers

Bodily/Kinesthetic: Surgeon, Athlete

Logical/Mathematical: Scientist, Engineer

Visual/Spatial: Artist, Architect

Interpersonal: Manager, Teacher

Intrapersonal: Coach, Minister

Verbal/Linguistic: Comedian, Lawyer

Musical/Rhythmic: Musician, Conductor

Naturalist: Landscaper, Forest Ranger

"Choose one career and write three (3) ways you could bring **peace** to the job."

_____

_____

_____

_____

_____

School Violence...Calming the Storm

Fight-Free Contributions

Objectives

To explore the fight-free contributions of famous persons identified in the categories of Multiple Intelligences.

To involve students in fight-free activities involving Multiple Intelligences by creating their own fight-free contributions in each of the areas of intelligence.

To demonstrate students' awareness of their own development in one or more of the areas of intelligence. If they choose a career in that intelligence, how would they make a fight-free contribution to society? How do they see working on that intelligence now as helping them later?

Materials

Introduce the student to the Multiple Intelligences:

- *Verbal/Linguistic*
- *Logical/Mathematical*
- *Musical/Rhythmic*
- *Visual/Spatial*
- *Interpersonal*
- *Intrapersonal*
- *Bodily/Kinesthetic*
- *Naturalist*

Generate samples of activities that represent each intelligence. Students, during discussion, might make a list of activities. From the list have students take a survey of the class to see which students feel proficient in one specific area. "Make a graph representing the results and discuss why a certain category would have more than another. Think about one of the intelligences in which you feel you are least proficient or with which you have the least experience and discuss what you could do to exercise that intelligence. Be ready to share your newfound intelligence the next day in class or write about it in your Fight-Free Journal."

Dr. Margaret R. Dolan

Research Activities:
Verbal/Linguistic

Objective

To research a famous person with Verbal/Linguistic Intelligence.

Procedure

"Famous people in this category include:

- Mark Twain - humorist, author
- Jesse Jackson. - minister, politician, speaker
- John F. Kennedy - politician, author, speaker
- Will Rogers - comedian, humorist
- Judith Viorst - author, humorist
- Maya Angelou - poet, play write, author
- Eleanor Roosevelt - speaker, diplomat."

Discuss information that students might already know about the famous persons listed. Students, individually or in groups, will choose one person to research.

"After researching the person, give examples of the person's contributions with the fight-free theme in mind, e.g., John F. Kennedy as President delivered a famous inaugural speech that empowered citizens to do for their country. As an author, he wrote a book entitled **Profiles in Courage** and **Why England Slept**."

To present findings from research, students might use a news show or Dateline format to share information. In so doing, students experience first-handed Verbal/Linguistic intelligence. Videotaping this presentation and sharing with parents or other classes, students could check-out the video each night to take home and show to their families.

School Violence...Calming the Storm

Research Activities:
Musical/Rhythmic

Objectives

To research a famous person who exhibits Musical/Rhythmic Intelligence.

To share works from individuals who have written songs of peace.

To compose a a fight-free song.

Procedure

Begin the lesson by discussing the famous persons, adding more to the list:

- Andrew Lloyd Weber - musical song writer
- Ella Fitzgerald - vocalist
- Grace Bumbry - opera soloist

Discuss the importance of people on this list to serve as fight-free role models.

"Choose a person in this category to research. Share your findings." *If students have access to the recordings of individuals, they may share.*

"In groups or as individuals, share a song of peace with the class." (E.g., *From a Distance, Let There Be Peace On Earth.*) *Students can perform the songs or bring in recordings.*

The class can work together to create a fight-free song. The McNair School song is to the tune of "You're A Grand Old Flag."

Dr. Margaret R. Dolan

Research Activities: *Logical/Mathematical*

Objective

To research a famous person who exhibits Logical/Mathematical Intelligence.

Procedure

Begin the lesson by discussing such famous persons as:

- John Napier - Scottish mathematician; invented logarithms
- Mae Jemison - Chemist, astronaut
- Marie Curie - French physical chemist; Nobel prize for chemistry.
- Barbara McClintock - Nobel Award for gene discovery

Discuss what students already know about the people on the list. Add to the list.

Choose a person to research. Present your findings. "How could this person contribute in a fight-free manner to society today with their intelligence in the areas of logic and math?"

"Choose a person in the area of logic and math who lived in the past. With information on their contributions from the time they were alive, think of how they would respond if they were to visit your school today. How would they use their talent to represent a fight-free message?"

"Represent the number of fight-free days by a graph, ratio, or percentages."

Have students create "If/Then" statements, exercising their logical thinking skills, using what they already know about Fight-Free Schools. E.g., if students learn peaceful problem solving now, then they will contribute to society as peaceful citizens in the future.

If students are attending school and are afraid for their safety, then it is hard for them to concentrate on learning.

School Violence...Calming the Storm

Research Activities:
Visual/Spatial

Objective

To research a famous person who exhibits Visual/Spatial Intelligence.

Procedure

Begin the lesson by discussing such famous persons as:

- Claude Monet - French landscape painter
- Frank Lloyd Wright - architect
- Benjamin Banneker - architect who designed Washington, DC
- Gabrielle "Coco" Channel - French clothing designer

Discuss what students already know about the people on the list. Add to the list.

"Choose a person to research. Present your findings. How could this person contribute in a fight-free manner to society today with their intelligence in the areas of art, illustration, and design?"

Have students discuss the contents of museums, using artistic expressions. Have students create a Fight-Free Museum. Students can brainstorm lists of things they would find in the museum. Categorize the list. Have students, in cooperative learning groups, choose a category and create the contents they would put in the Fight-Free Museum.

Dr. Margaret R. Dolan

Research Activities: *Bodily/Kinesthetic*

Objective

To research a famous person who exhibits Bodily/Kinesthetic Intelligence.

Procedure

Begin the lesson by discussing such famous persons as:

- Ben Franklin - inventor
- Michael Jordan - basketball player
- Dorothy Hammill - ice skater
- Florence Griffith Joyner - track and field runner
- Fred Astaire - dancer

Discuss what students already know about the people on the list. Add to the list.

"Choose a person to research. Present your findings. How could this person contribute in a fight-free manner to society today with their intelligence in the areas of dance, sports, or working with their hands?"

Have students discuss how they might organize a Fight-Free Olympics. "How would we ensure that professional sports such as baseball, basketball, and football are Fight Free?"

School Violence...Calming the Storm

Research Activities:
Intrapersonal

Objective

To research a famous person who exhibits Intrapersonal Intelligence.

Procedure

Begin the lesson by discussing such famous persons as:

- Dr. Martin Luther King, Jr. - minister, civil rights leader, speaker
- Helen Keller - author, lecturer
- Maslowe - psychologist
- Mahatma Gandhi - human rights and spiritual leader

Discuss what students already know about the people on the list. Add to the list.

"Choose a person to research. Present your findings. How could this person contribute in a fight-free manner to society today with their intelligence in the areas of human rights, spiritual awareness, and compassion."

Have students discuss what a fight-free, prejudice-free, humanitarian society might be like.

Dr. Margaret R. Dolan

Research Activities:
Interpersonal

Objective

To research a famous person who exhibits Intrapersonal Intelligence.

Procedure

Begin the lesson by discussing such famous persons as:

- Phil Jackson - professional basketball player, coach
- Henry Kissinger - political scientist, ambassador
- Franklin D. Roosevelt - politician, past U.S. President
- Andrew Young - mayor, ambassador, politician

Discuss what students already know about the people on the list. Add to the list.

"Choose a person to research. Present your findings. How could this person contribute in a fight-free manner to society today with their intelligence in the areas of working with others, negotiating, and teamwork?"

Have students generate a list of questions they might ask the person if he/she came to their school. "With a partner, role play the questions and responses the person might make."

Multiple Intelligences and Fight Free

Objective

To reinforce the fight-free message through the Multiple Intelligences.

Procedure

Students will use the Multiple Intelligences categories and project a fight-free message from a certain career perspective.

"'When I grow up, how can I use the Multiple Intelligences in sharing a fight-free message with the world?' Can you identify the intelligence you would use? Think of other careers that would match the intelligence identified and share how a person in that career would give a fight-free message to the world."

Dr. Margaret R. Dolan

Examples	Intelligence Used	Your Contribution
	VERBAL/LINGUISTIC	
KHFAAOOTY Talk Poem (see poem).		Create your own Fight-Free Poem.
	LOGICAL/MATHEMATICAL	
Draw logical conclusions about problems of conflict. How would you negotiate a peaceful solution?		Career: For my Fight Free message I would...
	VISUAL/SPATIAL	
Design a Fight-Free coloring book.		Career: For my Fight-Free Message I would...
	MUSICAL/RHYTHMIC	
Write a peace song or be a singer like Whitney Houston and sing "The Greatest Love of All."		Career: For my Fight-Free Message I would...
	INTERPERSONAL	
Be a psychologist and help people learn ways to solve problems peacefully.		Career: For my Fight-Free Message I would...
	INTRAPERSONAL	
Interview people and discuss how it feels to work or live in a community where people resolve their problems peacefully.		Career: For my Fight-Free Message I would...
	BODILY/KINESTHETIC	
Create a dance.		Career: For my Fight-Free Message I would...

School Violence...Calming the Storm

Section VI
Additional Resources

Dr. Margaret R. Dolan

"Big Wheeler Award"

presented to

for Outstanding Bus Behavior

_____ Teacher

_____ Date

_____ Bus Driver

_____ Principal

Nobel Peace Prize

presented to

_____

for Outstanding Efforts in Keeping the Peace

_____
Teacher

_____
Principal

_____
Date

Certificate of Membership

This certifies that

_____

is a member of the KHFAAOOTY Fight-Free Club.

You are responsible to follow the KHFAAOOTY pledge at all times.

Use KHFAAOOTY talk (please, thank you, pardon me).

Use a Write-Not-Fight form to solve a problem you are having with someone.

_____
Principal's Signature

KHFAAOOTY Bear

KHFAAOOTY Pledge

I pledge to keep hands, feet, and all other objects to myself.

I will treat others with respect in word and deed.

FIGHT FREE SCHOOLS

This certificate verifies

_____
School Name

as a participating
Fight-Free School

honors

_____
Student's Name

as a Fight-Free Student
on this day

_____

"Fight-Free School Day"

The mission of the Fight-Free Schools Program is to teach the youth of today, the future leaders of our nation, appropriate interpersonal skills. The focus is to provide an improved school environment which will enhance the learning process and allow our children the optimum advantage to excel in their academic careers.

Dr. Margaret R. Dolan

Ticket-To-Peace
WRITE-NOT-FIGHT

ADMIT ONE

I will be a peaceful citizen in my community. To keep the peace, I can use this ticket. If someone is making me angry, I can get help with the Ticket-To-Peace System.

I'll give this ticket to:

AND I will tell them about the problem.

(Use the back of this Ticket to help you Write-Not-Fight and get the help you need.)

Ticket-To-Peace

My Name: _____   Phone Number: _____

Address: _____   City and Zip: _____

I am having a problem with _____

_____

Who? _____ Where? _____ When? _____

I have tried these things: _____

_____

I am upset because: _____

_____

To solve the problem, I will ask my parents, my principal, or the police to help me.

School Violence...Calming the Storm

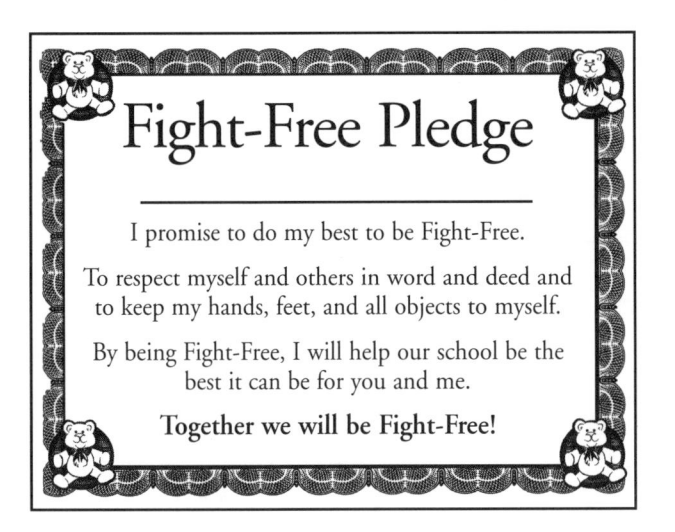

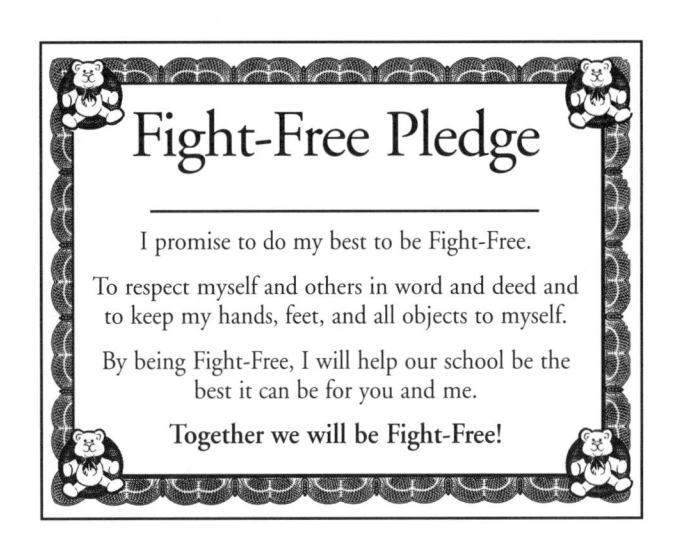

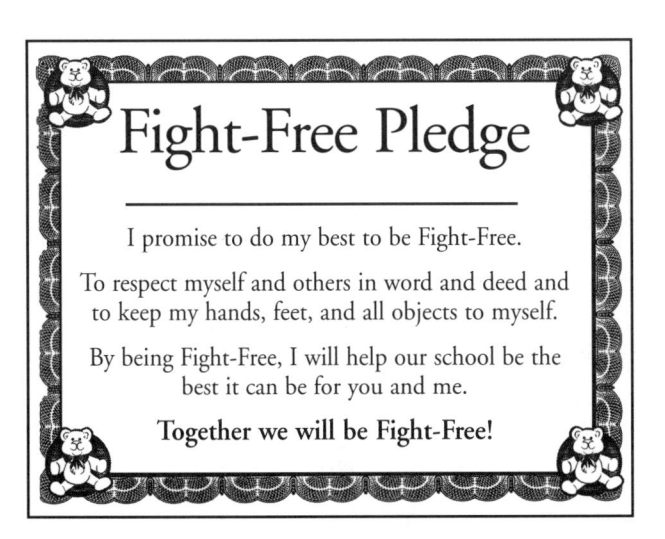

Fight-Free Pledge

I promise to do my best to be Fight-Free.

To respect myself and others in word and deed and to keep my hands, feet, and all objects to myself.

By being Fight-Free, I will help our school be the best it can be for you and me.

Together we will be Fight-Free!

Dr. Margaret R. Dolan

Fight-Free Song

Fight Free is Where I Wanna Be

By Scott Taylor
Principal, Orchard Farm Elem.
St. Charles, Missouri

Fight Free is where I wanna be Fight Free for all to see. Fight Free when the world gets tough for me I wanna be fight free

VERSE 1 What do you do when someone is pushing you? What do you do when you're out at play? What do you do when the feeling comes over you I wanna be fight free.

Vs. 2 When you wanna hit and when you wanna swing your fist What do you do to stay fight free? You walk right away and you don't even take the time I wanna be fight free

VERSE 3 We're from (own school) fight free is where we'll be With our fight free flag for all to see We're proud of our school + what it means to you and me I wanna be fight free (repeat 2 times)

School Violence...Calming the Storm

Fight Free is Where I Wanna Be
(Fight-Free Song)

By Scott Taylor
Principal, Orchard Farm Elementary
St. Charles, Missouri

CHORUS
Fight Free is where I wanna be
Fight Free for all to see
Fight Free when the world gets tough for me
I wanna be Fight Free

VERSE 1
What do you do when someone is pushing you
What do you do when you're out at play
What do you do when the feeling comes over you
I wanna be fight free

REPEAT CHORUS

VERSE 2
When you wanna hit and when you wanna swing your fist
What do you do to stay Fight Free
You walk right away and you don't even take the time
I wanna be fight free

REPEAT CHORUS

VERSE 3
We're from Orchard Farm (own school) Fight Free is where we'll be
With our fight-free flag for all to see
We're proud of our school and what it means to you and me
I wanna be fight free

REPEAT CHORUS

Dr. Margaret R. Dolan

Parmer Lane Elementary's Fight-Free Flag.

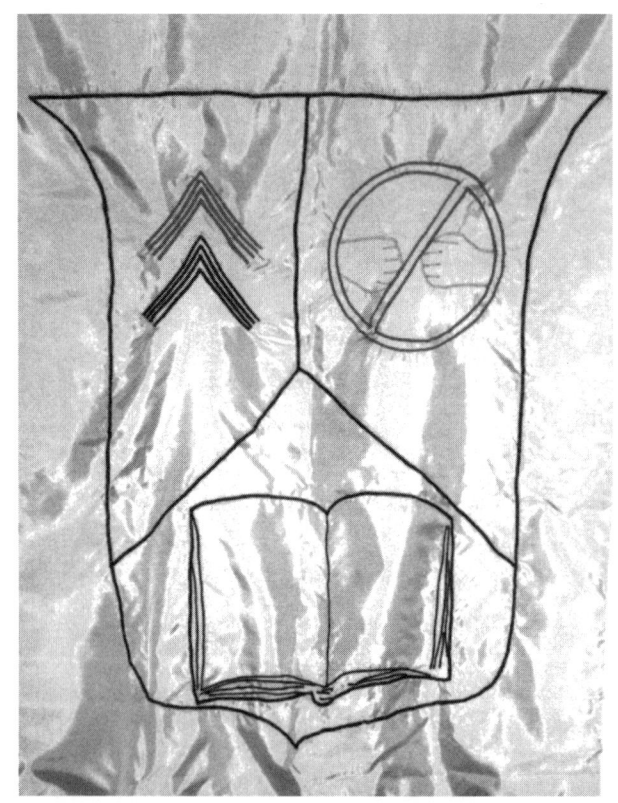

McNair Elementary's Fight-Free Flag.

❖Students Rise to Fight-Free Expectations❖

by Dr. Margaret R. Dolan, Ph.D.

EDUCATION St. Louis   **May 1993**

This article is dedicated to all of the McNair Elementary students in the Hazelwood School District.

As an educator, I am aware of the successful endeavors of the Drug-Free Schools Program, and I am proud to say, as principal of McNair Elementary School in the Hazelwood School District, that we have a successful drug free environment. We host a variety of drug education and prevention activities, yet as principal of grades K-6, I found the office referrals weren't for drug problems, rather the referrals were for pushing, kicking, hitting, or as more commonly termed on the discipline card "fighting." As I received the discipline referrals for fighting, I would perform my Judge Wapner duties. I investigated, gathered witnesses, and determined appropriate consequences sending the offenders off with the plea, "Go and fight no more." However, the next day I would have the same "fighting" referrals, repeat offenders, and mounting detention and suspension assignments. This is not to say that violence was running rampant in our school. Most students responded casually to Judge Wapner with, "Oh, we weren't fighting , we were just playing around." Or they responded, "Well, we were play fighting and it turned into a real fight." And even more popular was the line, "He/she hit me so I hit back"...and justice reigned in the students' minds. In determining a course of action, I reviewed successful programs in our school and why they were effective. The Drug Free concept was an astounding success. The attractions to the Drug Free Program was that everyone was involved in a positive approach to become aware of the consequences of using drugs in a harmful manner and to learn behaviors that would prevent drug abuse.

I took my lead from there and attempted to excite the entire school with the concept that if we were drug free we could be fight- free too, and here is what we were going to do to become fight- free. I announced at the end of the school day to our 520 students that we had 516 who were fight free. My office staff cheered, and the Fight- Free campaign was launched. The next day, the end of school announcement was, "Congratulations to all of McNair's 520 students who are fight-free." Since most campaigns have slogans, banners, ribbons, and buttons, I promised the students we would fly a "Fight-Free Flag" everyday we were fight- free. So excited was I to fly a "Fight- Free Flag" that I created one myself. The staff unanimously declared that it resembled a surrender flag. However, that did not deter me from running it up the flag pole. Unfortunately that afternoon, a storm blew the flag to shreds. The students were very accepting of my lack of Betsy Ross skills, and one talented student, Brad Oberle, volunteered to create a new Fight-Free design. Our PE teacher, Ruth Wise, was successful in sewing a flag that now hangs in our second floor window. I ordered red ribbons in our school color for all 520 students, and the gold lettering read, "I'm a Fight-Free Wildcat." I told the students if they could remain fight free until our first Red Carpet recognition ceremony on October 11, they would each receive a ribbon. I gave out 520 ribbons that day. Also at that time, each classroom received a large "We're a Fight-Free Classroom" ribbon. If a student hits, kicks, pushes, or shoves, the classroom ribbon is taken down that day. If there is an actual fight, with two people hitting each other, the school flag is taken down. The Fight-Free campaign continued with daily announcements applauding fight-free students and offering reminders for alternative behaviors to fighting.

In January, I conducted a positive behavior workshop in two assemblies, one for primary and one for intermediate. The students enjoyed the reading of *The Principal from the Black Lagoon* by Mike Thaler, pictures by Jared Lee, published by Scholastic, Inc. The book tells the story of a boy who gets sent to the principal's office and sits in the waiting room imagining the horrors that await him. Once inside, the principal's office is not the dungeon he imagines, and the principal instructs him to apologize to the teacher for accidentally bumping the wig off of her head with a broom.

This humorous story led to a discussion on feeling safe in the principal's office and the importance of being honest about the behavior that won the student the visit. Students often want to tell the other person's behavior as validation for what they have done. I tell the students they are in charge of their own behavior. The students had an opportunity to brainstrom on large sheets of craft paper with titles such as: "What does a good school look and sound like?" Then breaking it down to: "What does a good cafeteria look and sound like? What does a good playground look and sound

> *"I suggested instead of fighting they could seek adult mediation, intervention, have a cooling off period, count to ten, or put a picture in their head of not fighting."*
> -Dr. Peggy Dolan

like?" I reviewed our rule, as I do at the start of each day to keep us fight-free reminding them to..."Keep hands, feet, and all other objects to yourself." Students are invited to put a picture in their head of a fight-free day at McNair.

Also at the behavior assembly, students verbalized that they do become angry at other students. I suggested instead of fighting they could seek adult mediation, intervention, have a cooling off period, count to ten, or put a picture in their head of not fighting. The urge for validation often leads the student to take the law into their own hands to help them maintain a sense they are having their day in court. A worksheet was prepared and labeled, "The Write Not Fight" form. The student could communicate to the teacher what their problem was, why they were angry, and who was involved. This would tip the teacher off to a potential problem and provide a sense of being heard from the student in a conflict situation. Some students felt a fight was okay if they were hit first. Yet I told them to seek assistance and there would not be a fight. The message was comprehended because I began to receive referrals for one person hitting, kicking, or punching.

The students have been motivated to stay fight-free by the positive recognition they have received from the Hazelwood School District Superintendent, Dr. Larry Humphries, and Hazelwood Mayor, David Farhquarson. Our sixth grade cheerleaders even have a special Fight-Free cheer. Parents have supported this program and commented on several occasions that when the first fight of the year occurs, it will be a rough day at McNair.

At this writing, we have had a total of three fights this year. Last year in my annual report, I recorded twenty-seven suspensions for fighting (suspensions are a consequence for second offense fighting). On March 19, when the Fight-Free Flag was taken down, one of our students said to her mom, "Did the principal really expect that there wouldn't be a fight all year?" The mother replied, "Yes, and so did everyone else."

The Fight-Free Program is aligned with the school's goal of providing a positive school climate which will enhance academic achievement. Students share a feeling of pride in the fight-free status. The Fight-Free Program is also a strategy used to meet the goals set by teachers to allow students to become more responsible for their own behavior. The school is involved in a school-wide assignment notebook program with its own set of incentives. Staff efforts in developing learning interventions for students to feel success in school adds yet another component to the positive self-esteem exhibited by McNair students. Large banners greet students in the hall declaring, "Excellence Begins With You", "I'll Be A Success", "Best Teachers- Best Students-Best School", and "Believe, Achieve, Succeed." Expectations and accolades for students are visible and audible with daily public announcements from the principal.

As you drive by our school, we announce to the community that we are fight-free with a flag and an attachment to our school marquis heralding, "MCNAIR ELEMENTARY - A FIGHT-FREE SCHOOL." We expect it to remain that way.

❖Community Rises to Fight-Free Expectations❖

Education St. Louis   *by Dr. Margaret R. Dolan*   March/April 1994

Clues For A Fight-Free School

This article is dedicated to the almost 20,000 Fight-Free students enrolled in the program.

In May of 1993, the headline in *EDUCATION St. Louis* read, "Students Rise to Fight-Free Expectations." That headline referred to McNair School's 520 students, in the Hazelwood School District, that they were Fight-Free. The students announced to their neighborhood that they were a fight-free school by flying a flag everyday they were fight-free.

A few minor editing changes will be necessary to report what has occurred in one year. The new headline reads, "Community Rises to Fight-Free Expectations." And in the story, the number of 520 has been changed to almost 20,000 fight-free students participating in the Fight-Free Schools program. Here is the math problem of the day: How do you go from 520 students to almost 20,000 in less than one year? Here are some clues to help put the pieces of the fight-free picture together.

CLUE NO. 1:

EDUCATION St. Louis Magazine published, Angela Wexelman, supported the concept and published the article, "Students Rise to Fight-Free Expectations" in May of 1993. The article states how at McNair Elementary School a 94.5% drop in fights resulted when students participated in the Fight-Free Schools Program. The program combines incentives for non-violent behavior and alternative methods to communicate anger. It provides positive reinforcement in the form of rewards for students who do not fight, while at the same time, it teaches written and verbal conflict management. To create a climate of fight-free expectations, every morning the principal makes announcements over the public address system congratulating the school for having "X" number of fight-free students. A special Fight-Free Flag is customized by each school and flown each day that the entire school does not have a fight. Every classroom also has its own trophy size,"We're a Fight-Free Classroom" ribbon. Student are given individual ribbons as membership in the Fight-Free program.

If a student is involved in hitting, shoving, or kicking another student, the classroom ribbon of the offending student is taken down for a day. If there is an actual fight, with two people hitting each other, the school's Fight-Free Flag is taken down by the students involved in the fight. At some point throughout the school year, the principal conducts positive behavior workshops for the entire school.

CLUE NO. 2:

St. Louis County Executive, Buzz Westfall, listened and believed in the commitment of an elementary school principal's idea to stop violence at the elementary level by waging a campaign called Fight-Free Schools. Mr. Westfall hosted a breakfast and invited elementary school principals to also listen. An important piece to this part of the puzzle is that Mr. Westfall decided to sponsor this program before 1993 left us with two young school aged girls abducted and murdered. His support came before a summit on violence was called and before any money was released from the Classroom Safety Act, which promises a windfall of millions of dollars. His support has published newsletters, grant proposals, videos, and mailings in response to the daily inquiries that are received in the County Executive's Office. The program has expanded to almost 20,000 enrollees with a sum of zero dollars in the treasury.

CLUE NO. 3:

Principals representing every county district, public, private, and parochial schools attended the breakfast Mr. Westfall sponsored and they admitted that it was time to address the issue of fighting in schools in a positive manner. Those who committed to adopting this program were able to make site-based decisions with school committees solving problems for ways the program would be most effective in their schools. The diversity and the creativity employed by principals in implementing their plans can be found in the sharing fight-free tips as reported in the newsletter entitled, "On the Fight-Free Front." Since the program is not a lock step approach, the sharing of ideas has generated a resource for principals exploring the concept. Thanks to principal Rob Sainz, at Carmen Trails Elementary School, we now have an official mascot. The principal took the one fight-free rule - "Keep Hands, Feet, and All Other Objects To Yourself" and made the acronym KHFAAOOTY. A 'KHFAAOOTY Bear" visits the primary classrooms reminding them of the one important rule to keep them fight-free. Another school dedicated their non-violent efforts to two students who were victims of shootings while another school promised Ozzie Smith as a reward for meeting fight-free goals. These principals have discovered what makes the Fight-Free Program work...a collective positive effort that permeates the school, allowing the academic setting to be the most conducive to optimum learning. They have reported a decrease in fights and when a fight does occur, it is less severe. Rick Krietner, principal of Jury Elementary School, states, "In all of my experience as an educator, I have never experienced a program that effected such a positive change in behavior so profoundly. Staff and students have changed their expectations - we now expect there won't be a fight!"

A special thanks to Superintendent Dr. Larry Humphries and Assistant Superintendent Dr. Gene Reynolds, of Hazelwood School District, who promoted Fight-Free efforts. The have worked toward its expansion and they encourage school leaders to support the Fight-Free Mission Statement..."To teach the youth of today, the future leaders of our nation, appropriate inter-personal behavior skills. The focus is to provide an improved school environment which will enhance the learning process and allow our children the optimum advantage to excel in their academic careers."

CLUE NO. 4:

St. Louis County Police Chief, Colonel Ronald Batelle, believed in the concept and offered the assistance of the police force. Officer Tony Coleman is now the official Fight-Free Cop on the Beat. Through his efforts, we have produced two videos in conjunction with the program. One of the videos is on Fight-Free Schools and the other entitled, "Protect Your Child," features safety tips for children when strangers approach them. This video was shown on television in the St. Louis viewing area. Officer Coleman spoke to parents at a Forum on Violence urging them to become involved in their school's effort in combating violence and teaching appropriate inter-personal social skills.

CLUE NO. 5:

Parents have supported the schools' efforts by offering financial assistance through their PTA/PTO efforts. Principals can count on them to help provide the ribbons, flags, or bumper stickers that say, "My child attends a Fight-Free School." The response from parents is positive. Some parents have encouraged Fight-Free Families to reduce sibling rivalry they were experiencing.

Are you adding the clues to get the big Fight-Free picture of how we went from 520 to 20,000 students? With the high level awareness of the rise of violence in our nation, the response seems to be top heavy in treating the problem. Are more prisons and more police really the only answer? Recently, as I attended a Fight-Free Flag raising at Point Elementary School, I informed the 615 students that they were now part of the 898 from University City, 527 from Ritenour, 1,343 from Pattonville, and 1,500 from Parkway. As math lessons go, if we keep adding our numbers, what will this mean for our community in the future? One brave student raised his hand and said,"It will mean that we have a lot of people not fighting." With that thought in mind, I commend the efforts of the participants in the Fight-Free Schools Program, and I urge us to continue the team effort for Fight-Free Schools and Communities.

Dr. Margaret Dolan is principal of McNair Elementary School in Hazelwood School District and President of Fight-Free Schools, Inc.

❖ THE FIGHT-FREE FRONT ❖

Issue 3   Fall 1995

We Can Help Stop Violence Through the Fight-Free Schools Program!

FROM THE RING LEADER:
by: Dr. Margaret R. Dolan, President of Fight-Free Schools, Inc.

How many students in your school did not fight today? How many students in your school did not hit a teacher today? I'll bet my Fight-Free flag that your number not fighting is the larger number. I even venture to say that in the schools that are experiencing the effects of the escalation of students using physical aggressive behaviors, there are still more students who do not fight and that's the behavior that we want to become the expectation in our schools. While speaking at the kick-off assembly at Jefferson School in Normandy School District, a young student asked me what I thought of that boy in the news who hit his teacher. Before I could reply, he stated emphatically, "My mama said I better not be hitting on my teacher." Out of the mouths of moms to babes comes a large portion of the solution to how do we stop violence in the schools? BEGIN TEACHING NON-VIOLENCE AT HOME! The Jefferson student had a head start on the lesson of the day. However, what do we do when the parents don't teach the lesson at home? Does this tie our hands for the job we have to do at school? We all know the difficulty we face as educators when we can only address part of a student's problem when we do not have home support. Schools around the nation are facing this issue, and many districts have formed task forces to study possible solutions especially regarding violence in schools

In my review of studies, I have found that the programs that work in schools are programs that work on prevention and take a more proactive approach to changing student behavior as opposed to punishing inappropriate behavior when it happens. Nothing new under the sun about that approach; however, when the violence in schools, that used to be another district's problem, is now at our school door we can become overwhelmed and miss the simplest of solutions. A metal detector at the front

FIGHT-FREE IS THE RIGHT PRICE FOR SCHOOL BUDGETS - IT IS FREE AND IS YOUR PROGRAM WHEN YOU ADOPT IT!

door will only serve to quell a panicked public for the moment, however the long term effect of changing student behavior is the single most important tool we have in winning the war on school violence. Fortunately, the same newspaper that reports the school violence stories reported recently that another school joined the Fight-Free ranks, and the principal from Avery School reported that since starting the program she has seen a dramatic drop in the number of children getting into fights and conflicts and being sent into the principal's office. "They're doing different things than just hitting back."

Since working on the Fight-Free Front, I have been asked what is the number one cause of fighting in schools. Not surprising to principals, it is something as simple as butting in line or the dreaded "drive by elbow". In a local high school recently, where a fight broke out, the newspapers were quick to ask if the fight was racially motivated. Hats off to Principal Frank McCallie who stated, "The fight began because some students butted in line." Whether elementary or secondary, lines are unavoidable, and "butting" is a universal practice. One of the lessons in the behavior workshop conducted with the Fight-Free program role playing is what to do when someone butts in line. One seemingly clever second grade student bit someone in line because they "butted". His response to me was, "Well, I knew you'd take the flag down if I hit him." My response was the one rule, "Keep hands, feet, and all other objects to yourself, and that includes teeth", along with the administration of a consequence from our Code of Conduct.

When asked if the Fight-Free Program will work in high schools, it makes me wonder...if the causes of fights are the same, aren't the solutions?

Backing any fight-free effort is the Code of Conduct book given to all students and parents clearly stating consequences for inappropriate behavior. In addition to the fight-free daily messages, school flag, classroom ribbons or banners, and individual ribbons, buttons, or medallions, behavior workshops serve to teach and applaud appropriate interpersonal social skills. Such tools as mediation teams, Write-Not-Fight forms, or Tickets to Peace are used to give students an avenue to use their cognitive thinking skills which is a more powerful tool than might in solving problems.

My fight-free travels have taken me to schools of every demographic make-up, size, both private and public. I have discovered that we're all in this together and just as violence is a universal language, so is the language of peace and that's the word we spread in fight-free schools. Hats off to all of the principals who have implemented fight-free and are now in their second and third years. They are spreading the word to other schools.

Principal Dave Benyo in Kansas City has workshopped four schools in his area, Beulah Newhardt is retired and still spreading the word in Springfield, MO. Sarento, IL spread the word and Attorney General of Indiana spread the word when grant money became available. Joe Pokalinis in Grand Rapids, Michigan said five or six schools have now started Fight-Free since he shared the information. Joe sums up his opinion of Fight-Free by stating the aspect he appreicates most about Fight-Free is that it gives kids an opportunity to walk away and save face. At his school, he reports, "It's not cool to fight any more." Keep cool in Grand Rapids!

In the next issue, I'll share government involvement in the Fight-Free Arena.

ATTITUDE ADJUSTMENT

Orignial words and music by Leotha Stanley. Verse 3 and this arrangement of lyrics by Lisella Martin from Jefferson Elementary School.

We all need an attitude adjustment

Sometimes I think I'm shrewd, sometimes I can be rude.
Lookin' for a conversation where I can intrude.
Then I looked in the mirror and I said, "HEY DUDE!"
What you need to do is adjust your attitude.

We all need an attitude adjustment
 (2 times)
I really thought it over and found it plain to see.
How I react to what you do is certainly the key. (THE KEY)

So if you ever do me wrong, I won't come unglued. I'll count to ten and say why not adjust my attitude.

We all need an attitude adjustment.
 (2 times)

REFRAIN:
Just fine tune the times when you might,
Disrespect another, argue, fuss, or fight.
The choice is up to you and it won't take long.
Adjust your attitude, you know right from wrong.

We all need an attitude adjustment.
 (2 times)

Fight-Free at Jefferson, OH YEAH!
You know we gotta keep that banner flying high! (FLY HIGH!)
Stand up for yourself, but DON'T FIGHT, USE YOUR HEAD, think about it and do what's right.

ADJUST YOUR ATTITUDE!

TRY A LITTLE ATTITUDE ADJUSTMENT!

We all need an attitude adjustment.
 (2 times)

REFRAIN

We all need an attitude adjustment
 (2 times)

REFRAIN

We all need an attitude adjustment
 (2 times)

A T T I T U D E - ADJUST MY ATTITUDE.
A T T I T U D E - ADJUST MY ATTITUDE.
A T T I T U D E - ADJUST MY ATTITUDE.
A T T I T U D E - ADJUST YOUR ATTITUDE.

JUNIOR HIGH AND MIDDLE SCHOOLS BECOME FIGHT-FREE:

Thanks to Assistant Principal Dave Kew, Sperring Middle School in the Lindbergh School Distrtict, the fight-free word is being spread. Dave is in the third year at Sperring Middle School with 1275 students and reports a drop in fights since the program was implemented. Students are divided into teams by grade level and each team flies a Fight-Free Banner in the commons area. If students fight, the banner is taken down during the time of the suspension. Components that are a part of this middle school plan are: a code of conduct, a conflict resolution program, daily score card, and incentives germane to the age level of the students in the program. Students earn points on a score card kept by the assistant principal for no tardies, no office referrals, and no fights. At the end of a two month interval, winning teams receive such incentives as sandwiches from Subway.

Dave has shared his success with other middle schools, and he sounded great on KMOX in October when he was interviewed by Charles Jacobs. A fight-free salute to Dave and thanks for helping to keep the middle and junior high school flags flying.

Assistant Principal Patricia Peele from Hardin Middle School in St. Charles School District, reports that the Hardin committee of teachers is doing the ground work at present and have taken their cue from Dave Kew and have reduced fighting and office referrals. They are currently working on a timeline with a second semester goal as the kick-off. They are working from a teacher generated list on community members who would provide incentives or recognition. The students will be entering a contest to design the flag. Patricia states that the teachers feel that this is a proactive approach to add to the conflict resolution program already in place. To help this program become more student driven, they are discussing Tickets to Peace being available in the classrooms. A Ticket to Peace will be included in this mailing. They are use-

THE FIGHT-FREE FRONT

Welcome Aboard: Hoech Middle, Sperring Middle, Hardin Middle - Fight-Free Flags are Flying High!

ful to send home to involve parents in getting the message to the home front. The best of luck to Hardin Middle. Dr. Dolan will be speaking to all of the principals in St. Charles School District in January and will keep us posted on Hardin's progress.

FIGHT-FREE AT JUVENILE JUSTICE SEMINAR.

St. Louis County Juvenile Justice Association invited Fight-Free Schools to speak at their annual fall seminar. Assistant Principal Elaine Walden from the Mehlville School District at Bierbaum School opened the session sharing her fight-free success stories at two schools. When Elaine was at Point Elementary, she was instrumental in starting the fight-free program and that led to her beginning the program at her new assignment. Elaine shared that her PTA gave a $50 United States Savings Bond to the student who created the winning design for their Fight-Free Flag. A fight-free salute to the Mhelville Schools who are keeping the peace by flying the Fight-Free Flag each day.

Current Enrollment Status:

FIGHT-FREE TID BITS
Upcoming Fight-Free Workshops and Seminars

MCSA - Missouri Council of School Administrators:
November 29 - Springfield, MO
December 6 - Kansas City, MO

MAESP - Missouri Association of Elementary School Principals
Spring Conference

NAESP - National Association of Elementary School Principals
March Conference

DARE National Conference - August

United States: 26 states
Nova Scotia
South Africa
Approximately 100,000 students

FIGHT-   FREE

Fight-Free Featured on KETC "Mosaic" which airs on November 28 at 7:30 pm

FAMILIES: While being interviewed on KMOX radio, Dr. Dolan was asked by Barbara Whiteside if she could do Fight-Free with her children at home. Dr. Dolan talked with her school's PTA and they agreed that maybe the following easy and fun things to do might help those times of sibling rivalry in the family. Just think...peaceful solutions to: who sits by the window, whose turn is it to take out the trash cans, whose socks are you wearing?

Starting with the Family Survey, then follow the examples from our booklet to learn about the Family Meeting, Family Fight-Free Pledge, Family Write-Not-Fight Form, and the Family Crest. There is a family fun page and newsletter page you can share at school.

Dr. Dolan's school sent a family booklet of suggestions home last year, and maybe you'd like to make your own booklet to send home.

FIGHT-FREE SURVEY:
1. Our family time of tension occurs most often in the: ___AM ___PM
2. Where? ___at the table ___playing ___in the car ___in a room of the house ___other
3. What are the top three reasons we do not get along? (Example: phone time, chores, toys)

---

4. What three things can we do to make these times better?

FIGHT-FREE FAMILY MEETING
After everyone in the family has an opportunity to write out a Fight-Free Family survey, arrange for a Family Meeting and remember...a Fight-Free Family meeting should include ALL IN THE FAMILY (sure, pets are allowed too).
1. Someone should be the chairperson of the meeting.
2. Someone should take notes so you remember about the meeting.
3. The chairperson will read survey results.
4. Discuss ideas and ways to solve #4 on the survey.
5. Write you plan.
6. Arrange celebrations at the end of a Fight-Free day, week, or month.
7. Sign the Fight-Free Family Pledge and place it on your refrigerator.
8. Design your Family Fight-Free Crest and fly it on your refrigerator each day you are fight-free.

WRITE-NOT-FIGHT FORM
At school, when we are faced with fighting to solve a problem, we try these things...
1. Stop and think and picture another way to solve the problem instead of fighting.
2. Use a Write-Not-Fight Form
3. Seek help from someone else so that we can talk it out.

WRITE-NOT-FIGHT FORM
Name: _____
I am having a problem with _____.
Who: _____ When: ____
Where: _____
I have tried these things_____
I am upset because _____
To solve the problem I am going to _____
FIGHT-FREE FAMILY PLEDGE
We, the _____ family, will observe the Fight-Free rule..."Keep

Page 3

Share Your Song, Pledge, Tip, Poem...

Hands, Feet, and All Other Objects to Yourself." We will celebrate being fight-free and fly the Fight-Free Flag on our refrigerator.

Family Signatures
(each person in the family should sign)

_____ _____

FIGHT FREE FAMILY CREST

Family Name
The Divisions of the Crest are the Peace Symbol.
Fill in section 1 with a picture of your family.
Fill in section 2 with the first names of your family (or draw one).
Fill in section 3 with your family motto (Ex. "All for one, One for all."

FIGHT FREE FUN PAGE
Use these spaces to draw a picture or write about the following:

What does a fight-free fight-meal look like?

What does a free car pool look like?

What does a fight-free family shopping trip look like?

What does a fight-free end of the day look like?

FIGHT FREE FAMILY NEWSLETTER ITEM
The _____ family would like to share its family fight-free crest.

We celebrate being fight-free by ____

Something special that happened at our family meeting _____

Other fight-free information to share __

WREN HOLLOW ELEMENTARY:
by Barbara Dunkman

September 12 marked the Bennet/Whitney Violence Free kick-off at Wren Hollow School. To celebrate the 3rd year of being violence free, the entire school assembled and sang "Lean On Me." Principal Mike Cerutti led the staff and students in saying the school's personal pledge. Wren Hollow's guest speaker, Dr. Peggy Dolan, gave an inspirational speech before the new classroom violence free banners were given out.

Each year that the Bennet/Whitney Violence Free Program has been implemented, Wren Hollow has experienced fewer fights. Everyone is looking forward to another successful year.

WELCOME NEW FIGHT-FREE SCHOOLS:
Lewis and Clark, Riverview Gardens School District (the St. Louis Rams visited their kick-off)

St. Blaise, St. Louis Arch Diocese

Prase Elementary, Granite City, IL

Holy Trinity, St. Louis Arch Diocese

Jefferson School, Ritenour School District

Elementary West, Wentzville, MO

TEXAS SCHOOL SUCCESS
Linda Rowold, Principal of Pamer Lane Elementary School in Austin, Texas, wrote Dr. Dolan recently praising the Fight-Free program she began in her school two years ago. She writes: "We had some challenging times getting started, but have seen very good results. Fighting has nearly become a thing of the past in our third, fourth, and fifth grades."

She goes on to say that she was informed that grant money was available for programs addressing justice issues through the Texas Bar Association. She is exploring the possibilities of providing both students and staff training in conflict resolution and mediation.

Her students have gone from wearing a badge daily to having Celebration Fridays when all fight-free students wear their fight-free friendship bracelets.

Thank you, Linda, for that great fight-free success story.

SEND US YOUR FIGHT-FREE SUCCESS STORIES
Included in this newsletter is a Fight-free Front Newsletter Item form. If you would like to share a news flash, song, tip, poem, pledge, or item with us, please fill it out and send to:

Dr. Margaret Dolan
Fight-Free Schools, Inc., President
McNair Elementary School
585 Coachway Lane
Hazelwood, MO 63042

A FIGHT-FREE SALUTE TO...Buzz Westfall who sponsors the Fight-Free Newsletter.

Fight-Free Schools, Inc.
Dr. Peggy Dolan, President
Molly Bunton, Vice President
Ellen O'Sullivan, Secretary
Mortimer J. Reilley, Board Member

❖ THE FIGHT-FREE FRONT ❖

Issue 4   Winter 1996

"Keep Hands, Feet, and All Other

FROM THE RING LEADER:
Dr. Peggy Dolan, President of Fight-Free Schools, Inc.

By the time you receive this newsletter, Random Acts of Kindness Week will have passed. I hope by designating one week to the concentration of kind words and deeds, that we don't miss the opportunity to promote and applaud acts of kindness everyday. Instead of reading headlines about drive-by shootings, wouldn't it be comforting to read about some drive-by kindnesses out there. Let me take this opportunity to run by some drive-by kindnesses that have been extended to the Fight Free Schools program...try these headlines...

* BUZZ WESTFALL CONTINUES TO SUPPORT FIGHT-FREE THROUGH SPONSORING THIS VERY NEWSLETTER!

* GRAND RAPIDS, MICHIGAN POLICE CHIEF PURCHASES FIGHT-FREE BANNERS FOR CLASSROOMS!

* RETIRED MAJOR LEAGUE UMPIRE, DAVE PHILLIPS, OFFERS HIS SERVICES AS MOTIVATIONAL SPEAKER FOR HARDIN MIDDLE SCHOOL'S FIGHT-FREE KICK-OFF...LEE HAMILTON ELEMENTARY HAS HIM BOOKED NEXT!

* RIVERVIEW GARDENS BASKETBALL TEAM AND CHEERLEADERS VISIT FIGHT-FREE STUDENTS AT LEWIS AND CLARK ELEMENTARY!

* KETZ, CHANNEL NINE AND KSDK, CHANNEL 5 HIGHLIGHT

FIGHT- FREE EFFORTS IN JANUARY!

* WEEKLY READER COVERS FIGHT- FREE IN AN APRIL ISSUE, 1996. POST DISPATCH COVERS FIGHT- FREE AT AVERY SCHOOL IN WEBSTER GROVES!

* NATIONAL ASSOCIATION OF ELEMENTARY SCHOOL PRINCIPALS ACCEPTS PROPOSAL (THIRD TIME IS THE CHARM) FOR FIGHT-FREE TO PRESENT AT THE NATIONAL CONVENTION IN WASH., DC!

* MIDDLE SCHOOLS JOIN RANKS OF FIGHT-FREE IN 95-96, SPERRING MIDDLE SCHOOL'S ASSISTANT PRINCIPAL DAVE KEW ASSISTS IN THE EFFORT.

I'm sure in your school setting you can add some drive-by kindness headlines of your own. Our headlines for fight free grow by the day as calls come in requesting information or reporting a fight free success story. Who ever said "success breeds success" has the perfect description of what happens when schools share their fight free stories with each other. Please take the time to share your story with us. I am impressed daily by the efforts of administrators around the country who are taking seriously the national education goal of 2000..."By the year 2000, every school in the United States will be free of alcohol and other drugs, violence, and the unauthorized presence of firearms and will offer a disciplined environment conducive to learning."
National Education Goals

FIGHT FREE WHO'S WHO

Government Sponsor: County Executive, Buzz Westfall

Fight Free Board of Directors.
Dr. Peggy Dolan-President
Mrs. Molly Bunton-Vice President
Mrs. Ellen O'Sullivan-Treasurer
Mr. Mortimer J. Reilley-Director

Welcome Aboard...

A Fight-Free Flag is getting ready to fly in Springfield, Illinois at the Jefferson Fifth and Sixth Grade Center. Cathy Sanders reports that everyone is enthused about the plans and students are working on an in-school television show to be used to teach the students appropriate interpersonal social skills. What a great way to get the message across of, **"KEEP HANDS, FEET, AND ALL OTHER OBJECTS TO YOURSELF."** Students will be the stars of the show and act out scenes that contain appropriate ways to handle the drive-by elbow in line or the hassling on the playground. She said they have not officially started the program; however, they have placed the Write Not Fight forms in the classrooms and the good news is...they are being used. So there is more to Fight-Free than just flying the flag. A fantastic start for Jefferson School...we're rooting for you!

POLICE ON PREVENTION PATROL:

Recently the Hazelwood School Board approved a pilot program that will use St. Louis County Police Officers as resource personnel at school sites. One police officer will be assigned to each of the three high schools. These officers will be stationed at the high schools but will be available to nearby junior high schools also. One purpose for this program is to have the officers get to know

Fight-Free And Proud! NATIONWIDE NEWS

the students and build a level of trust so that students will talk with police in an effort to avert problems. Sgt. Maggie Clayton, of the St. Louis County Police, reports for example that she had a high school student come to her and say the student witnessed someone stealing money from another's purse on the school bus. Officers on the spot can intervene.

At Hardin Middle School, in St. Charles School District, Assistant Principal, Pat Peale reports the use of their police department coming to school when students reported there was to be a big fight at the gas station after school. Students involved talked with the police and worked out solutions that did not involve fighting. In one instance, a neighborhood fight was averted at the school and after school. The police worked in a preventative manner and students could further build rapport and trust with the police seeing them in a different light. The police used to just show up after the fight. Being there all the time might help prevent the fighting. School Districts who currently are participating in the School Resource program are Mehlville, Parkway, and Rockwood and Hazelwood.

OUT OF TOWN FIGHT- FREE GUESTS:

Recently a delegation from Sibley Elementary School in Grand Rapids, Michigan visited Fight-Free School's President, Peggy Dolan. Two school principals and their resource policeman were among the visitors who are implementing the Fight-Free Program in their schools. The police officer works hand-in-hand with school personnel and students. He has become a fixture at the school. The officer reports that not only has fighting been drastically reduced, but students are talking to him freely about potential problems and he is serving as mediator when conflicts arise. They sent the following article:

FIGHT-FREE AT SIBLEY ELEMENTARY

Sibley Elementary is the first school in Michigan to embark on a unique and collaborative effort with the Grand Rapids Police Department entitled, "Fight-Free School." This is a proactive, violence prevention program that seeks to ensure a safe and non-threatening environment for all students.

As a result of Police Chief William Hegarty's financial and moral support, each classroom (19) was provided its own "Fight-Free Flag" prominently displayed outside each room. In addition, the school has a large similar flag which flies below the American flag outdoors. Each day that there is no altercation before, during, or after school, the flag is raised and a student announcement made. "Good morning students. Sibley Elementary is fight free for ____ days. the flag is up!" Students are responsible for raising the flag and the daily intercom announcements.

As a visual reinforcement, a large bulletin board hangs outside the playground entry door. This allows students and visitors to Sibley to be continually aware of the number of ongoing "Fight Free" days in our school.

Classrooms that remain fight free for a designated time period (10-12 weeks) are rewarded. Incentives have been as diverse as pizza parties, a magician, or popsicles with a free recess period. Principal Joseph Pakalnis reports a dramatic (75%) decrease in playground incidents and fight-related suspensions.

In the event of a fight, both the classroom flag and the building flag are taken down for a day by the building principal, the "consecutive day" count starts over, and the students announce that there was a fight and the flag is down.

Although Sibley is regarded as a high needs city building which services many "at risk" students, the results have spoken for themselves. Since the inception of the program on December 2, 1994, there has been only one fight amongst any of the 150 sixth graders! Peer pressure, along with providing alternatives to violence, and the ability to save face, has allowed students to "buy into" the concept.

Two major factors in the success of the program have been the SAP (Student Assistance Program) and the Peer Mediation Process. The Student Assistance Program has provided students with long-term help in coping with a variety of school and family concerns. SAP chairperson, Mary Ann Lowing, has noted an increase in both parent and student self-referrals since the inception of the "Fight-Free" concept.

Through the Peer Mediation Process, students now actively seek out student playground conflict managers to help resolve differences in a non-violent manner. As of November 7, 1995, Sibley Elementary had experienced only two fights in the third grade! This was largely due to the 124 student mediations that had been performed up to that date. Sponsors report that out of that number 113 (91%) were successfully resolved.

By working together, the community, staff, student body, and Police Department have made great strides in creating the "safe and orderly environment" at Sibley Elementary that all schools seek to establish!

MCSA SPONSERS FIGHT-FREE SEMINAR MAY 7, AT JOE HANNON'S BETWEEN 9AM AND 3PM

Middle Schools Come On Board! HOORAY!

THREE CHEERS FOR MIDDLE SCHOOL/JR. HIGH FIGHT-FREE-ERS

Thanks to retired professional umpire Dave Phillips, the students at Hardin Middle School enjoyed a rousing kick-off message to their Fight-Free program. With the help of Assistant Principal, Dave Kew, Sperring Middle School, the staff at Hardin were able to make some site based decisions in drafting the Fight-Free Program to meet their school's particulars needs. Pat Peale, Assistant Principal, reported during her Channel 5 news coverage that most effective was the zero tolerance stand on fighting. A strict Code of Conduct automatically suspending those involved in a fight drove the message home to students who are looking forward to their big reward day at the recreation complex in St. Charles.

HERE'S THE HARDIN PLAN:

Purpose:
The purpose of the Fight- Free Schools program at Hardin School is to decrease fighting and office referrals while increasing conflict mediation and resolution.

Components:
(1) Team Banners: Each team will have a banner displayed in the cafeteria during times when the team members are fight free. If a team member fights or assaults someone, the flag will come down for the period of the suspension (OSS). Our goal is to have all banners displayed each day. Banners will be provided for each team. A school Fight Free logo will be selected from student designs submitted during a contest which will be announced soon.

(2) Daily Points: Each team will have an opportunity to earn daily points. The possible number of points will vary according to grade level. The decision to scale the points in this manner is due to the significant difference in daily discipline per grade level.

Grade	6	7	8
Fight Free	5	6	7
Office Referral Free	5	6	7
Possible Points Daily	10	12	14

(All points will be tracked and tallied in the office.)

Repeat offenders (3 office referrals) will be placed on an individual contract aimed at addressing the inappropriate behavior. During the time on contract, that student will not be considered part of the program in terms of earning points or taking part in the awards. When the student has fulfilled the contract, he/she will be allowed back into the program to earn points and to enjoy the awards.

(3) Awards:
Level I: Whenever a team accumulates 120 points, the next day they will be awarded a coupon which will entitle them to go to the front of the cafeteria line for priority service and they will receive a "treat" at the end of the food line.
Level II: At the 5 week point in the quarter, the highest point team, per grade level, will receive a coupon for a food/beverage award in the cafeteria.
Level III: At the end of the quarter, the highest team will receive an extra special award. Possibilities include an extra special treat in the cafeteria or a field trip to the Rec-Plex or to a Cardinal's game. This level award will be determined at a later date. Any suggestions for an award or recommendations for a funding source are greatly appreciated.

So far, we have a donation of $200 from the Hardin PTA and $33 from the Drug Free grant.

Random Acts of Recognitions:
Along with announcements on point averages at regularly scheduled times, there will be random acts of recognition throughout the program. We are trying to arrange for visits to our school by public figures who would be willing to spend 15-30 minutes of their time to sign autographs or visit the classes with the highest scores on a given day.

The staff and students of Hardin Middle School held their Fight-Free kick-off assembly on January 13, 1996.

A BIG FIGHT FREE THANKS TO RETIRED UMPIRE DAVE PHILLIPS

**A PUBLICATION OF FIGHT FREE SCHOOL INC.
NEWSLETTER SPONSORED BY: BUZZ WESTFALL**

HOECH MIDDLE SCHOOL
(Project Peace)

Here's the Plan:
1) Semester Rewards:
   1st - Snow Ski Day at Hidden Valley
   2nd - 2 contests - one from the 2 man team and 1 from the 4 & 5 man teams
(2) Any student who has not been sent to the office will be put in a drawing and 200 students will go to the Cardinal baseball game during the school day.
(3) Monthly team winners receive a soda at lunch.
(4) Every 6 weeks (same as our grading system) we have an hour of co-curricular where teachers sign up for an activity. The students choose an activity. Ex: Roller blading, computer, cartoons, making lace bears, making beaded bracelets, basketball, etc. In all there are 30 activities.

Team Daily Points:
(1) no office referrals
(2) no time outs
(3) no bus referrals
(4) good behavior in morning and at lunch
(5) banner staying up (no suspensions from fighting)

A FIGHT-FREE THANKS TO LARCH FARRELL, OF MCSA, WHO HAS SPONSORED FOUR FIGHT-FREE SEMINARS IN MISSOURI FOR 95-96

ST. LOUIS COUNTY POLICE

The SAFE Schools Hotline
CALL
889-SAFE

SAFE HOTLINE:

Installation of a SAFE Schools Hotline phone number, which will allow students or their parents to report information confidentially regarding drug dealing or use, gang activities, violence, weapons, or other issues of concern was announced in January, 1995. By dialing the number, 889-SAFE, an individual can report information to, but not have to be face to face with law enforcement or security officers. All calls are answered electronically, monitored by the police department and will remain anonymous. Tom Hamlin Director of Hazelwood School District Security reports the program in its second year, is working well and effective when used.

Do you have a school Fight-

For information on the Fight-Free School program, send a self addressed stamped manilla envelope to:

**Dr. Peggy Dolan
McNair Elementary School
585 Coachway Lane
Hazelwood, MO. 63042**

**Free Pledge, Song, Motto or Symbol to share? We'd love to print it.
Send to Dr. Dolan today.**

We want to be sure you are a Fight-Free school, so fill out the verification form below and mail it today!

FIGHT-FREE VERIFICATION FORM

_____
(School Name)

_____
(Address)   (phone)

Number of Students: _____

Our Plan Includes:
* Daily:_____
_____
_____
_____

*Individual:_____
_____
_____
_____

* Classroom:_____
_____
_____
_____
_____

*Schoolwide:_____
_____
_____
_____
_____

_____
Signature of Principal

Mail to: County Executive's Office
Mrs. Rosemary Reisse
41 S. Central
Clayton, MO 63105

·The Fight-Free Front·

Fall 1996   October

President Clinton Endorses the Fight-Free Program!

FROM THE RING LEADER:
Fight Free Greetings! Those of you in the ranks of Fight Free will agree with me that when the President of the United States writes about Fight Free Schools, it is front page news. The President's nod for national recognition finds us that much closer to our goal of Presidential recognition for individual students who remain Fight Free for the tenure of their elementary, middle, and high school years. Because of the positive response of schools implementing the Fight Free program, government leaders such as Buzz Westfall, County Executive, and Congressman Dick Gephardt have been instrumental in forwarding the Fight Free proposal for Presidential recognition. The proposal is now in Secretary of Education Riley's office, and in the near future I will be going to Washington D.C. to confer on the details of this project.

Another project for Fight Free in the works is the planning of Fight Free Scholarships available to high school seniors who have maintained a pristine conduct record in their academic career. Students will be required to write an essay on how they will contribute to society as a peaceful citizen. I will keep you posted on these developments.

Bountiful thanks to all who participated in the 1995/96 Fight Free Evaluation. You provided valuable feedback and some input for future newsletters. Thanks to the efforts of University of Missouri Communications Intern, Peggy Clarke, we now have some statistics. Our goal will be to continue to track each year and accumulate the data for better evaluations. I appreciate the suggestions and recommendations and will be sharing many of the ideas with you through the newsletters. Once again, I invite you to share your songs, pledges, cheers, and kudos with us. Be looking for some of your successes in the Fight Free manual entitled, *School Violence...Calming the Storm,* scheduled for an early 1997 release with the Rising Sun Publishing Co.

I'll close with a brief summary from

> *"I concur that efforts to reduce violence among young people are much needed across our Nation."*
> -President Bill Clinton

our Fight Free Schools. Sixty-six principals surveyed said....

1. When principals were asked what the data indicated to them:
- 28.1% Decrease in fights;
- 18.8% Program is effective;
- 12.5% Positive impact on school environment;
- 12.5% Students aware of alternatives to fighting;
- 9.4% We need to work on it;
- 9.4% Helps kids resolve conflicts without fighting;
- 9.4% Transfer students are a problem.

2. When principals were asked what observations they considered to be the most indicative of the Fight Free Schools making a difference in their school's climate:
- 30.8% Can see it in the children's expression;
- 20.5% Positive peer pressure;
- 17.9% Increased awareness;

Remember to send in your Fight Free Verification Form for 1996/97.

- 17.9% Increased pride;
- 12.8% Calmer environment.

3. When principals were asked what they considered the greatest strength of the program:
- 33.3% Provides alternatives to fighting;
- 24.2% Greater awareness of Fight Free options;
- 12.1% Students taking ownership of their behavior;
- 12.1% Program offers a positive focus;
- 9.1% Increase in school pride;
- 9.1% Students thinking before acting.

4. When principals were asked what they considered the greatest weakness of the program:
- 29.3% Can't think of one;
- 22.0% Parents encourage kids to fight back;
- 17.1% Lack of clear definition of a fight;
- 17.1% Staff's inconsistent implementation;
- 14.6% The program is time consuming.

5. When principals were asked what unique problems they encountered:
- 30.8% Staff agreeing on definition of a fight;
- 19.2% Lack of parental support;
- 19.2% Initial staff buy-in;
- 15.4% Repeat offenders;
- 15.4% Poor staff follow through.

6. When principals were asked what

"Big Mike" Carries the Fight Free Message

unique features evolved from the use of the Fight Free Schools program in their school:
- 30.6% Fight Free parties;
- 25.0% Individual Fight Free awards;
- 25.0% Fight Free pledges, slogans, songs, etc.;
- 19.4% Fight Free special events.

7. When principals were asked if they would be interested in sharing their program with another school that wants to be Fight Free:
- 89.8% Yes;
- 10.2% In the future.

8. When principals were asked for further comments and suggestions:
- 50.0% The program works;
- 28.6% Thanks to Dr. Dolan;
- 7.1%   Program must be adaptable to each school;
- 7.1%   Students are learning Fight Free program;
- 7.1%   Program needs community support.

Here's hoping your Fight Free Flag is flying!   Dr. Peggy Dolan

FIGHT FREE ASSEMBLY:
Looking for that assembly to offer students that will carry your Fight Free message and serve as an incentive at the same time? *Big Mike and Company* have just the offering. Big Mike reports that his assembly, **"Fight Free Forever"**, was inspired after he read about the Fight Free Schools Program in the St. Louis Post-Dispatch. It is a kids course on conflict resolution! Five steps that help change fists that fight into hands that help. Each step has a hand motion that helps provide a visual cue for memory retention. The final lesson on forgiveness drives home Big Mike's call for kids to make their schools Fight Free...Forever! You might be interested in several other assembly selections which would also tie into the Fight Free theme. Other assemblies include: *The*

The White House
Washington
July 3, 1996
Dear Mr. Leader:
  Thank you for writing to inform me of the success of the Fight Free Schools Program. I concur that efforts to reduce violence among young people are much needed across our Nation. The Program's record in reducing the number of physical and verbal fights is impressive and I commend their work.
  I also agree that appropriate national recognition should be provided to promising programs such as these and have requested that Secretary of Education, Richard Riley, explore ways this can be accomplished and respond to you directly.
  Thanks for taking an interest in this important program. I look forward to continuing our work together in an effort to make America a safer place for children.
  Sincerely,

  Bill Clinton

The Honorable Richard A.
Gephardt
Democratic Leader
House of Representatives

Just Say No Show, I Dare to Care, and Play it SAFE. For more information write to: Big Mike and Company, 1241 New Towne Rd., Arnold, MO 63010

FIGHT FREE BUSES ON A ROLL:
Townsend Elementary School students look forward to the bus ride to and from school thanks to the efforts of the bus drivers and school personnel. Townsend is continuing the Bus Safety Baseball Program initiated by Dr. Peggy Dolan, but with a new twist. In an effort to reduce the number of bus write-ups, Patrick Lee, Amy Collier and Beth McMillan have assigned a volunteer staff member to teach on the buses, serve as the "coach" and cheerleader, meet and greet the bus, ride the bus home, talk to students having difficulty, and generally support the driver in every way possible.

A student on each bus is the assistant coach and he/she works closely with the head coach.

The bus receives one run for each day that there are no write-ups to and from school. Students receive rewards as they earn 20, 40, 60, 80, and 100 runs. The cooperation between the staff, the bus drivers, and the students has been wonderful. (Townsend School is in the Hazelwood School District.)

HANDS FOR PEACE:
At Grannemann Elementary School, in the Hazelwood School District, students call their Fight Free Program, *Hands for Peace*. This year they have added, *Voices for Peace* to their Fight Free Program. Principal Rick Kreitner reported a decrease in fighting behavior with fists; however, name calling and verbal arguments continued. Daily announcements include words students will use that are peaceful and applauding students when they use peaceful conflict resolution words.

BISMARK ELEMENTARY:
The following Fight Free song was provided by Bismark Elementary School in Bismark, Missouri. Thanks, kids!

Fight Free School Song

Dance xx Shout xx Sing it all about!
We have a fight-free school.
Dance xx Shout xx Sing it all about!
We'll all obey the rules.

Come on everybody sing this song.
Join your hands and get along.
Fly your banner high in the sky.

MCSA Fight Free Workshop

♪♫ *Peace (Love/Joy) will reign if we try.*
Dance xx Shout xx Sing it all about.
We have a fight-free school.
Dance xx Shout xx Sing it all about.
We'll all obey the rules.

ST. BLAISE SINGS:

FIGHT FREE SONG
(to the tune of "Cheers")
Making your way in a school today takes everything you've got.
Taking a break from all your school-work sure would help a lot.
Wouldn't you like to get away?

Sometimes you wanna go where no one ever ever fights.
And they're always glad you came.
You wanna be where you can see our problems are all the same.
You wanna be where everybody feels the same.
You wanna be where people know that fighting is not right.
You wanna be where everybody feels the same.
Climbing the walls when no one calls you've lost, you fought again.
And the more you're down and out, the more you need a friend.
When you long to hear a kind hello.

FIGHT FREE SONG
(to the tune of "Felix the Cat")
It's amazing, it's remarkable, it is fearless, unbelievable.
It is super-dooper and extraordinary.
It's the kind of thing that keeps you feeling merry. What?
The fight free flag, the wonderful, wonderful flag.
Whenever we get in a fight, it helps us to do what is right.
The fight free flag, the wonderful, wonderful flag.
You'll laugh so much your sides will ache, your heart will go pit-a-pat Watching St. Blaise Fight Free Flag!

FIGHT FREE FLAG
F!GHT FREE SONG
(to the tune of "Addams' Family)
Fight Free!   Fight Free!
We're fight free and we know it.
At school we like to show it.
Don't start a fight and blow it.
The St. Blaise Family!
St. Blaise is the best.
The best in all the West!
So come and be our guest and join the family.
So always be fight free and come along with me,
The St. Blaise Family will

FIGHT FREE PLEDGE
We, the students of Townsend School promise to be fight free.
We promise to solve problems peacefully, respectfully, and cooperatively.
We promise to support one another as we strive to remain fight free.

FIGHT FREE PRESENTATIONS COMING UP...
Monday, Nov. 11, 1996
Inn at Grand Glaize, Lake Ozark, MO
Tuesday, Jan. 14, 1997
Blue Springs South High School
Community Rm., Blue Springs, MO

Registration Fee: $60.00
MASA or MAESP members: $50.00
(includes lunch and handout materials)

Make check payable and remit to:
MCSA Outreach
P.O. Box 1117
Columbia, MO 65205-1117

FIGHT FREE CONFERENCES WERE HELD...

August 7 and 8: Three Fight Free sessions were conducted at the National D.A.R.E. Conference in St. Louis.
August 20, 1996: Fight Free was presented at the St. Louis Arch-Diocesan Seminar.
September 26, 1996: MCSA Outreach sponsored a workshop at St. Charles Admin. Center in St. Charles, MO.

S.T.A.R. - STRAIGHT TALK ABOUT RISKS

While an unprecedented number of school-aged children are being injured and killed in gun related incidents, many educators may not have the resources to address this urgent issue. To meet the need for educational materials about the dangers of playing with or carrying guns, the *Center to Prevent Handgun Violence* has developed gun violence prevention programs for students in grades Pre-K-12, and their families.

Q: What is STAR?
A: STAR is the nation's premier gun violence prevention program for school-aged youth and their families. STAR is a primary prevention program, premised on the belief that all U.S. children and teens are at risk of gun injury or death. STAR is designed to help youth develop victim prevention skills and to rehearse behaviors needed to manage problems, such as conflict and peer pressure, non-violently without guns.

STAR materials include:
* Skill-building activities for grades Pre-K-12;
* Posters, hand-outs and other awareness materials designed to promote parent and community involvement;
* Age-appropriate bibliographies of literature and audio-vidual resources;
* Video presentations;
* National guide of complimentary

Straight Talk About Risks (STAR)

violence prevention programs;
* Inservice training materials;
* Spanish translations.

Q: Who researched and developed STAR?
A: STAR is based on academic and focus group research conducted by the *Center to Prevent Handgun Violence*, as well as a joint pilot project with the public schools of Dade County, FL. With this foundational knowledge, Center staff worked closely with teachers, guidance counselors, students and parents to write the curriculum. A team of national experts in child development, injury prevention, curriculum design, crime prevention and law enforcement provided critical review prior to STAR's publication in 1992.

Q: How many school systems are using the STAR curriculum?
A: STAR is being used by selected school systems: New York City, Los Angeles, Chicago, and Dade County, FL. STAR has also been effectively implemented as part of police led crime prevention initiatives, and in conjunction with recreation and health education programs.

Q: Why will STAR help to reduce gun deaths and injuries?
A: STAR is based on state-of-the-art primary prevention strategies. Prevention education that goes beyond simply raising awareness can reduce risks, by helping youth to develop social problem-solving skills and life-saving behaviors for use outside of the classroom.

Q: Aren't parents really the ones who need to learn about preventing gun violence?
A: Absolutely. Because parents play a major role in safeguarding their children from gun violence, STAR includes parent information. Parents need to ensure that guns are always kept away from children and teenagers. It is also important for parents to talk to their kids about the dangers of guns and the consequences of gun violence.

Q: How do teachers fit STAR into their already-busy teaching schedules?
A: STAR has a flexible format. STAR activities readily supplement health education and violence prevention programs. STAR is also suited for use with traditional subject area courses, e.g., language arts, science, or math.

Q: How is the STAR program funded?
A: STAR is entirely funded through private and public grants. Center staff work closely with schools and youth agencies to determine program needs and costs for STAR training and curriculum delivery.

Q: Is there a political agenda presented in STAR?
A: The goal of STAR is simple — *to reduce gun injury and death afflicting youth.* STAR does not promote a political or legislative agenda, nor does the program condemn well-supervised, controlled shooting sports or hunting.

Q: How do I get started?
A: Call the *Center to Prevent Handgun Violence* to request a review package of STAR materials. Then, develop a plan of action for your staff to receive training and to implement the STAR program. A full day of staff training is recommended to get started and can be arranged through the Center's STAR program office:

The STAR Program
Center to Prevent Handgun Violence
1225 Eye Street, NW, Suite 1100
Washington, D.C. 20005
Tel: (202) 289-7319
Fax: (202) 408-1851

FIGHT FREE VERIFICATION FORM

School Name _____

Address _____ Phone No.

Our Plan Includes:
*Daily:_____
_____
_____
_____

*Individual: _____
_____
_____
_____

*Classroom: _____
_____
_____
_____

*Schoolwide: _____
_____
_____
_____

Signature of Principal

Detach and mail to :
Dr. Peggy Dolan
McNair School
585 Coachway Lane
Hazelwood, MO 63042
(314) 839-9665

Fight Free Schools, Inc. Board

Dr. Peggy Dolan, President
Mrs. Molly Bunton, V. President
Mrs. Ellen O'Sullivan, Secretary
Mr. Mortimer J. Reilley, Board Member

The Fight Free Front

Issue 5　　　　　　　　　　　　　　　　　　　　　　　　　　　　　　　　　　Spring 1997

Fight Free Wins One of Twelve Best Practices in Missouri

From the Ring Leader:

In an effort to secure presidential recognition for individual Fight Free students, I went to Washington, D.C., to discuss the concept with William Modzeleski, Director of Safe and Drug Free Schools. As you may recall in the Fall Fight Free Front issue, Congressman Richard Gephardt sponsored the proposal to seek presidential recognition for individual students who are Fight Free and the President responded positively. The visit to Washington was to discuss concrete ways that recognition will take place. I will continue to keep you posted on the progress. I want to thank Congressman Gephardt and his assistant, Kathy Dente, for their support of Fight Free Schools.

As I shared with Mr. Modzeleski, due to the support of our government leaders, the Fight Free Schools program has spread and has influenced the lives of students. In the excitement of Fight Free being selected as one of the 12 Best Programs in Missouri, I was thankful for the support of County Executive, Buzz Westfall who was the first to give Fight Free a nod and sponsors our efforts to this day. I receive communication from schools that share with me that their mayor, state representative, council person, or congress person came to the school to talk to students and congratulate their Fight Free endeavors. It is the recognition of such leaders that serves as a motivation for students to continue using the strategies of non-violence that they are learning in the Fight Free program.

Look for the Cardinal Baseball ticket news on page 2. We have our dates set and look forward to the annual Cardinal support of the Fight Free program.

In this fifth year of Fight Free, I close with the wish that your Fight Free Flag stays flying.

Dr. Peggy Dolan

CONGRATULATIONS TO FIGHT FREE SCHOOLS PROGRAM:

The Fight Free Schools, Inc. program has been selected as one of the 12 Best Practices in Missouri through Success Link, a division of the Missouri Council of School Administrators. The Missouri Department of Elementary and Secondary Education is recognizing 12 validated, innovative programs that are effective in improving student performance. This effort is in response to the Outstanding Schools Act of 1993. Director of Success Link placed the winning call to Dr. Peggy Dolan, founder and President of Fight Free Schools, Inc. Dr. Schlichting reported that there were 167 entries. Success Link is responsible for recognizing, disseminating, and exchanging information about the best professional teaching practices and programs in the state. A resolution from the Missouri Senate will be given to recognize the Fight Free Schools program. Dr. Peggy Dolan wishes to thank all of the schools in Missouri and across the nation who have made a commitment to improve the interpersonal socials skills of students to assist in reducing violence in schools, one school at a time.

**HELP US - HELP YOU
CALL
The Safe Schools Hotline
889-SAFE
to report
Drug, Gang, Weapon
Violations
All calls are anonymous and confidential.**

889-SAFE HOTLINE UPDATE:

Two years ago, the Hazelwood School District Safety and Security Department implemented a special SAFE SCHOOLS hotline with all calls going to the St. Louis County Police headquarters in Clayton. The SAFE SCHOOLS hotline enables students and parents to call 889-7233 anytime and leave anonymous information about illegal criminal activity in our schools. Mr. Tom Hamlin, Hazelwood School District's Coordinator of Safety and Security, has been encouraged by the response. There have been 24 calls placed resulting in 23 suspect identified with six arrests. Categories of the calls were as follows: Sexual harassment, drug offense, assault, and weapons. Every student and parent is urged to immediately contact a teacher, school police resource officer, or administrator if safety is an issue. However, student peer pressure is much greater today; therefore, students are invited to call 889-SAFE with assurance of privacy if they do not feel comfortable discussing a security issue with an adult.

Mr. Hamlin advises anyone interested in setting up such a hotline in their school district to contact their local police department to design a working memorandum with the police. This will ensure appropriate communication when a hotline call is received.

Coming Soon: *School Violence...Calming the Storm*

FIGHT FREE MANUAL:

The Rising Sun Publishing Company will publish the Fight Free Schools, Inc. manual. The manual is entitled, *School Violence...Calming the Storm*. This manual will be available for spring publication. For ordering information, call 1-800-524-2813 or write to Rising Sun Publication, 4829 Fjord Pass, Marietta, GA 30068.

HIGHLAND MIDDLE SCHOOL:

Highland Middle School, in the Turner Unified School District No. 202, Kansas City, Kansas, reports that since they started the Fight Free program, fighting incidents are dramatically down from the past few years. Fred Haws, Assistant Principal, believes that since they started a more pro-active approach with Fight Free the students are finally aware that fighting is wrong. Better yet, if they don't fight they will be rewarded. Fred said, "The most impressive part of our program is the banners. Each team made a banner and hung it in the lunch room." In the first year of the program, fighting was reduced." Go, Highland Middle School, Go!

CAMDENTON UPPER ELEMENTARY SCHOOL:

The Camdenton Upper Elementary School, grades 4-6, has decided to become a Fight Free School. The Fight Free committee includes teachers, administrators, parents, and community members who have been planning for the past year to get ready to become Fight Free. The teachers have been training in Conflict Resolution Skills and have attended two Fight Free workshops. Planning sessions have also included the school's D.A.R.E. officer, the campus police officer, a member from the Chamber of Commerce, and other community organizations. With over 800 students and 50 bus routes, Assistant Principal, Cindy Gum, is confident they can overcome any problems that the large number may create. Other schools in the district have shown interest in the Fight Free program. Assistant Principal Gum is planning that their Fight Free program will be so successful that others in the area will want to implement it in their buildings as well. Let us know how you do, Camdenton. We'll be cheering for you!

SPERRENG MIDDLE SCHOOL:

Assistant Principal, Dave Kew, from Sperreng Middle School, sends a big thanks to Dave Sinclair Ford in St. Louis for adopting Sperreng and supporting their Fight Free efforts. This sponsorship has resulted in support for the incentives involved at Sperreng. Such incentives include visits from St. Louis Rams football players, a magician, free soda, and public relations efforts with the news media. Such community support is a vital component in the Fight Free program. The generosity of business partnerships offers assistance when already tight school budgets are earmarked for other areas.

CARDINAL BASEBALL TICKET NEWS:

Once again, thanks to the footwork of Marty Henden, the Cardinals have granted us 6000 Cardinal Baseball tickets. We will be given the opportunity to admit Fight Free students. Here's the scoop:

April 28, 7:05 pm - San Francisco
(2000 Fight Free guests)

April 29, 7:05 pm - San Francisco
(2000 Fight Free guests)

May 21, 12:35 pm - Pittsburgh
(2000 Fight Free guests)

If you are registered as a Fight Free School, in the St. Louis area, you will be contacted by Rosemary Reise in Buzz Westfall's office. She will give you the particulars on arrangements for entrance on the designated days.

Take me out to the ball game,
Take me out with Fight Free.
We're celebrating, so come join the spree,
Yeah, Fight Free's five year anniversary.
So mark the date and be ready,
Our flag will be flying high.
So, it's hands, feet, and all objects to self,
Cardinals love Fight Free.

FIGHT FREE HAPPENINGS

MCSA Sponsors Fight Free Seminars for 1996/97:

September 26, 1996
   St. Charles, MO
November 11, 1996
   Lake of the Ozarks
January 14, 1997
   Blue Springs, MO
April 8, 1997
   Cape Girardeau, MO

For more information contact Larche Farril at (573) 556-6272.

FIGHT FREE CONFERENCES
June 20, 1997
   Shrine of Our Lady
   of the Snows
   Belleville, IL

July 29-31, 1997
   Missouri D.A.R.E.
   Officers' Conference
   Tan-Tar-A
   Osage Beach, MO

KHFAAOOTY Takes SAT's...

KHFAAOOTY TAKES SAT'S:

Schools are always looking for ways to excite students regarding the standardized testing that schools are required to administer. To help create a positive testing climate, some Fight Free schools invited KHFAAOOTY Bear to be the star motivator. KHFAAOOTY, as you know, is the Fight Free Bear whose name means: **K**eep **H**ands, **F**eet, **A**nd **A**ll **O**ther **O**bjects **T**o **Y**ourself. KHFAAOOTY sat in a special desk in the hallway with an SAT answer grid, a number two pencil, and word bubbles that included testing tips for students. KHFAAOOTY suggested that students: Get a good night's sleep to prepare for tests, eat a good breakfast (you need brain food for your test), respect quiet zones for testing, and use a marker to help you stay on the right track.

Especially in the primary grades, students enjoyed seeing their Fight Free friend each day doing the things they were doing as they took their tests. Students received small tickets each day. On the last day of testing week, KHFAAOOTY and each student received a certificate for completing the week. We'll be waiting for the test results to come in, and we'll let you know KHFAAOOTY's I.Q...we already know he is 100% Fight Free! See page 4 for sample SAT KHFAAOOTY certificates.

FIGHT FREE FRONT STAFF:
Peggy Dolan
Molly Bunton
Linda Biernbaum

FIGHT FREE BOARD MEMBERS:
Government Sponsor: County Executive, Buzz Westfall

FIGHT FREE BOARD OF DIRECTORS:
Dr. Peggy Dolan - President
Molly Bunton - Vice President
Ellen O'Sullivan - Treasurer
Mortimer J. Reilley - Director

FIGHT FREE EVALUATION:

In partnership with the University of Missouri - St. Louis, Professor Al Madrid will be assisting Fight Free in acquiring an intern to assist with the annual Fight Free evaluation. An evaluation helps validate the Fight Free program with statistical data. Please assist us in this process when you are contacted in June concerning the Fight Free evaluation. Thank you for taking the time it takes to fill out the evaluation forms. The Fight Free program benefits by your participation in the evaluation process.

LET US KNOW:

What Fight Free information do you have to share with other Fight Free schools? Do you have a song, a jingle or a rap, an idea, an assembly, an incentive, a tip, a change, or a result? We learn from each other. Every conference or seminar that I present Fight Free, I find out something new and different that works for their school. Please send us your Fight Free news to include in future newsletters.

FIGHT FREE VERIFICATION FORM

_____
(School Name)

_____
(address)   (phone)

Number of students: _____

Our Plan Includes:
Daily:_____
_____
_____
_____

Individual: _____
_____
_____
_____

Classroom:_____
_____
_____
_____

Schoolwide:_____
_____
_____
_____

_____
Signature of Principal

Mail to: Dr. Peggy Dolan
585 Coachway Lane
Hazelwood, MO 63042

The Fight-Free Front

Issue 6   Fall 1998

Fight Free Manual Set For Publication Fall, 1998

From the Ring Leader:

Fight Free Greetings to all, and I hope your Fight Free flag is flying. My Superintendent, Dr. Humphries, came to visit our staff, and one of the first things he said was, "Tell the kids I asked if the flag was up." What a motivator it is to say to the student body that the Superintendent asked if they were Fight Free that day. It is that kind of motivational tool on which the Fight Free program relies. It sounds simple, however, the verbal praise given over the PA announcing that our Superintendent was proud of our 520 Fight Free students at McNair means so much to the students. Dr. Humphries was counting on the McNair Wildcats to keep all hands, feet, and all other objects to themselves. Keep those announcements coming daily.

You can imagine my surprise, as I sat at the Fight Free Cardinal game on May 21, when a fight broke out clearing the benches. We had 2000 Fight Free students in attendance, and as any educator would, I took full advantage of this baseball brawl to become a teaching moment. The crowd was chanting, "Fight, Fight, Fight!" Dr. Dolan announced to her Fight Free first grade students, "In Fight Free, we don't ever cheer for a fight!" One student responded, "We don't?" Dr. Dolan explained that maybe the team didn't know the Fight Free students were watching. The next day, students wrote letters to the Cardinals and gave them some of our Fight Free tips. Many editorials were printed the following week regarding the event and the need for the sports world to set an example for our youth. All the more challenging our job becomes in teaching peaceful means to solve a problem. The good news is that the two other games, where over 4000 more Fight Free students attended, were fight free. Have your students send thank you notes to Marty Hendin, Cardinal Baseball, 200 Stadium Plaza, for arranging our tickets last spring. We owe him a big thank you for his support of the Fight Free program. THANKS, MARTY!

There are lots of Fight Free announcements in the works. One big announcement is that Rising Sun Publishers tells me that the Fight Free manual is almost ready for press. I have included classroom activity pages which will help to give the principal an extra hand in keeping the Fight Free message in the forefront. You will find a great idea for each class to create a Fight Free Bulletin Board. Also included is a Fight Free Calendar with monthly activities for primary and intermediate classes. This year, to maintain focus, the McNair KHFAAOOTY Bear is represented on a sign outside each homeroom. Each sign shows that homeroom's Fight Free Goal. During announcements and class visits, I can discuss with students examples of ways they are working toward meeting their goal. We plan a celebration in January for goals accomplished and will set new goals for the second semester. You'll find these ideas and more in the manual. Give Rising Sun a call and check on the publication date. Call them at 1-800-524-2813.

Included in this newsletter are the evaluation results from the 1996/97 school year. Many thanks to all who returned the Fight Free Evaluation form. Several universities have called to ask if we had tracked any data on the program. Thanks to you, we now have two years of evaluation results which serves as statistical data that shows the Fight Free program is successful. Several doctoral candidates have requested the data to use in dissertations and promise to share their results with us. I will be sharing with you some of the ideas generated from the evaluation in this and future newsletters. A big thanks to our County Executive, Buzz Westfall, who continues to sponsor the Fight Free Newsletter. His support has carried us all the way to Washington D.C. where efforts are underway to provide Presidential recognition for Fight Free students. Congressman Gephardt is vigilant with this project, and I'll keep you posted on the progress.

Thanks to all who help spread the Fight Free word. By sharing your success with others, we invite more success in providing opportunities for others to provide the safe and orderly school environment so needed for optimal learning to take place.

Keep Your Fight Free Flag Flying!

Fight freely yours,
Dr. Peggy Dolan

Send Thank You Notes to:
Mr. Marty Hendin
St. Louis Baseball Cardinals
200 Stadium Plaza
St. Louis, MO 63102-1722

FIGHT FREE SEMINARS
As in the past, Larche Farril, Director of Missouri Council of School Administrators, is sponsoring Fight Free Seminars around the state. This August 11, Dr. Dolan and the Fight Free crew went to Columbia, Missouri, to spread the Fight Free word to 35 participants. Dr. Dolan thanks the Fight Free crew who gave of their time and talents so generously. A

Fight Free Seminar December 2, 1997

Fight Free salute to Densie Little and Mary Fischer of Hoech Middle School and Rick Kreitner of Grannemann Elementary School.

> **Future Fight Free Seminar**
> Dec. 2, 1997 - Warrensburg, MO
> Contact: Larche Farril
> (573) 556-6272

WEST HEART
Dr. Nancy Allison, Principal of West Elementary, in the Wentzville School District, reports that West Heart is a performing troupe that appeared at the 1997 MAESP convention. They promote topics such as teamwork, the importance of education, kindness, honesty, and leadership. They are very entertaining and are interested in performing in Fight Free assemblies. For more information, contact the band at (913) 851-0385. Dan Siewert is the National Tour Director.

PEACE EDUCATION FOUNDATION
Principal Rick Kreitner, Grannemann Elementary School, reports that he contacted the Peace Institute, and they have provided a three day training session for three staffers and curriculum materials for the entire staff. The topic is How to Make Peace Work. Rick says they are using materials to support their Fight Free program which is named "Hands for Peace." For more information contact:

Peace Foundation
1900 Biscayne Blvd.
Miami, FL 33132-1025

FIGHT FREE BAG OF TRICKS...
It's in the bag!
Here are some Fight Free ideas generated from the responses of the 1996/97 Fight Free Evaluation:
* We have a monthly assembly or fun activity for students with positive behavior and promote random acts of kindness with positive congratulation certificates and drawings for prizes.
* Fight Free students have the privilege of attending skating parties and dances.
* We have an end of the year field trip for students who are Fight Free the entire year.

Will Fight Free work at the junior high/middle school level? Contact our experts: Dave Kew, Sperreng Middle School, 849-0123 or Denise Little, Hoech Middle School, 426-9561.

* A "Design a New Flag" contest was held with the winners receiving saving bonds. The new flag was presented in the procession at the Mass of the Holy Spirit.
* Over the past four years, we have tried the school flag and individual classroom crests that illustrate individual classroom mission statements about how to be Fight Free. Now our Fight Free program has become part of our participation with Washington University and the "Total Quality School" program or movement in the St. Louis area.
* An award is given to those who have had good behavior during the year.
*We had a culminating year end activity called "Peace Week." This activity took place during the last full week of school. We had a myriad of peaceful activities including a Peace Drawing, a Peace Problem of the Day, etc. I would be happy to share details upon request. Principal Joyce Akridge, Mary E. Nicholson School, (317) 226-4270.
* Fight Free Activity day instead of an assembly: students chose as a class or grade level their own activities as a reward and reinforcement for being Fight Free. This was a whole day activity on a particular day at a particular time. The activities lasted about 45 minutes. Our school continually announces heroes of the day. Each week a staff member talks to the student body over the PA system about being Fight Free.

FROM THE KHFAAOOTY CORNER
Don Gruenwald, Principal of Fox Elementary School, in the Fox School District, reports that his school adopted a very large stuffed bear mascot which they named KHFAAOOTY. He wore the school t-shirt and even went to the ball game with the school on Cardinal Fight Free Night. Classrooms that were Fight Free all week got to have KHFAAOOTY spend an entire day in their classrooms. He got to sit with Fight Free kids and go everywhere they went in a red wagon. Believe it or not, even the 6th graders cheered when they heard their class announced on the intercom as the recipient of KHFAAOOTY for that day. Kids wrote him notes, made Fight Free pictures for him, and he was a great accessory to our Fight Free program.

"Miss" and "Master" at St. Joseph
Principal Mary Ellen Schraeder, from St. Joseph Elementary in Cottleville, boasts that her school has a "Miss" and a "Master" KHFAAOOTY. They are stationed in different classrooms

Fight Free Evaluation Summary, 1996/97

throughout the year. They attend each assembly and are a good reminder of the Keep Hands, Feet, and All Other Objects To Yourself rule.

ST. BLAISE SCHOOL SAYS...
Mary Tomaine, Principal of St. Blaise, tells us that they have a KHFAAOOTY bulletin board area in the school's main foyer. The number of consecutive days are proudly displayed there.

KHFAAOOTY JUNIOR
At McNair Elementary School, in the Hazelwood School District, a sixth grade student approached Dr. Dolan with the concept of KHFAAOOTY Junior. It seems sixth grade students were upset that Dr. Dolan only awarded KHFAAOOTY to the primary students. Sixth grade students brought it to the student council and came up with KHFAAOOTY Junior. Students purchased smaller bears for each classroom and named them KHFAAOOTY Junior. Each class has their own mascot, and the students thought it would be an opportunity for more kids to get to hold the bear for a day. Classrooms decide on who holds KHFAAOOTY Junior. Student empowerment in action!

FIGHT FREE FRONT STAFF
Peggy Dolan
Molly Bunton
Linda Biernbaum

FIGHT FREE BOARD MEMBERS
Government Sponsor: County Executive, Buzz Westfall

BOARD OF DIRECTORS
Dr. Peggy Dolan, President
Molly Bunton, Vice President
Ellen O' Sullivan, Treasurer
Mortimer J. Reilly, Director

FIGHT FREE EVALUATION 1996/97

Years Enrolled in Fight Free program	1 Yr = 10	2 Yr = 7	3 Yr = 9	4 Yr = 8	5 Yr = 4					
# Students Enrolled	100 or less 1	101 - 200 2	210 - 300 5	301 - 400 7	401 - 500 9	501 - 600 6	601 - 700 4	701 - 800 3	801 - 900 0	901 - 1000 1
My School is...	Private 3 = 8%	Public 31 = 82%	Parochial 4 = 10%							
Demographic setting	Suburban 25 = 66%	Urban 7 = 18%	Rural 6 = 16%							
Incidents of Fighting has Increased	0 - 20% 8 = 21%	20% - 40% 10 = 26%	40% - 60% 10 = 26%	60% - 80% 6 = 16%	80% - 100% 4 = 11%					
Number of times flag has come down	1 - 10 13 = 34%	10 - 20 6 = 16%	20 - 30 2 = 5%	30 - 40 4 = 10%	40 or more 9 = 25%	No flag yet 4 = 10%				
# Fight Free days	1 - 35 3 = 8%	36 - 70 7 = 18%	71 - 105 5 = 13%	106 - 140 12 = 32%	141 - 175 11 = 29%					

FIGHT FREE INDICATOR OF SUCCESS 1996/97

	No Influence	Somewhat of an Influence	High Degree of Influence	Very High Degree of Influence	No Information Available
Student Empowerment		11 = 29%	14 = 37%	9 = 24%	4 = 10%
Overall School Climate		2 = 5%	15 = 39%	20 = 53%	1 = 3%
Staff Involvement		8 = 21%	16 = 42%	13 = 34%	1 = 3%
Parent Involvement	3 = 8%	19 = 50%	11 = 29%	3 = 8%	2 = 5%
Use of Instructional Time	1 = 3%	11 = 29%	19 = 50%	4 = 10%	3 = 7%
Student Academic Achievement	2 = 5%	16 = 42%	10 = 27%	2 = 5%	8 = 21%

Fight Free at Keysor Elementary

FIGHT FREE AT KEYSOR

The following newspaper article was taken from the Webster-Kirkwood Times, May 30-June 5:

We are fifth grade students at Keysor Elementary School. We are writing to inform people about the Fight Free Program at Keysor. We think that this program has really made an impact on how kids solve their problems at our school.

McNair Elementary, in Hazelwood School District, was the first school to have the Fight Free program. Principal Peggy Dolan started it.

The program at Keysor began when our principal, Ms. Sapp, heard Peggy Dolan on the radio talking about the Fight Free program. Ms. Sapp talked to Mrs. Champion, our counselor, and they decided we needed something to help kids solve their problems without fighting. Ms. Sapp and Mrs. Champion called Peggy Dolan for information and suggestions.

Every Friday our counselor, Mrs. Champion, announces the Fight Free classrooms on our school intercom system. Twice a year all Fight Free students are acknowledged at an all school assembly. Each month, classrooms that have been "Fight Free" get certificates. Every class has a Fight Free Banner hanging in their room.

If a student in the class chooses to solve a problem with their hands other than their words, then the classroom's banner is taken down. Everyone tries harder to keep the banner flying.

This program has definitely increased the students' ability to solve problems in a Fight Free way at Keysor Elementary School. It has made our school a much calmer and safer place to learn.

**Maggie Creamer and
Kelly Schnitzmeier
Kirkwood**

FIGHT FREE PLEDGE
from Walnut Grove School

"I promise to do my best
to be Fight Free...
To be the BEST I CAN BE...
To respect myself and others too.
In all I say and do...
To be the BEST I CAN BE...
To keep my hands, feet, and all objects
to myself..
To be the BEST I CAN BE...
By being Fight-Free,
I will help Walnut Grove
To be the BEST IT CAN BE
For you and for me.
Together, as a family, we will be
FIGHT-FREE!"

**Walnut Grove School
Fight Free Kick-Off
Assembly
October 3, 1997**

IVELAND ELEMENTARY
Submitted by:
Charmaigne Scott, Principal
Iveland School

Iveland School's Fight Free program has been very successful for several years. The following information will let you know some of the ideas and practices that have worked in our program.

In September: Each class takes a Fight Free oath and signs a Fight Free contract. The contract is put on display outside the classroom door.

Weekly: Each teacher and staff member is responsible for making a Fight Free announcement. These are usually announced on Monday mornings. The announcement includes telling the "Heroes of the Day" (students who avoided a potential fight), how many consecutive days the school has been Fight Free, and a "pep talk" on a theme such as making good choices and being a responsible citizen.

On-going: We have a front hall display of classes that have been Fight Free for the whole month. If a class has been Fight Free for the whole month, a sticker is added to their banner.

On-going: Each class has a Fight Free flag outside their classroom door. If a fight occurs by students in their room, their Fight Free flag comes down for one day.

On-going: We have a tally chart in the cafeteria indicating how many Fight Free days our school has had in a row.

Quarterly: At the end of each quarter, we celebrate being Fight Free by having a Fight Free Activity Day. Students and teachers decide on a fun activity. These include: Movie and popcorn, board games, a softball game, free play outside, etc. The activity is held for one hour at the end of the day.

If students participated in a fight during the quarter, they do not join in the activity.

The Fight Free program at Iveland School has been very effective. We have 500 students in our program, and we are all committed to being "Fight Free."

STUDENT CONTRACT
We the undersigned agree to follow the guidelines of the Fight-Free School. We will not hit, kick, or throw things at another person. By following these rules our school will be a safer and happier place.

Iveland
——— ——— ———
Fight Free

◆ Fight Free Front ◆

Issue 7   March 1998

Fight Free Community Business Partnership - Church's Chicken

From the Ring Leader:
When you come aboard the Fight Free train, you soon realize that you need to partner with the community and link with area businesses. As well as area businesses supporting your fight free efforts monetarily, one thing rings loud and clear:

VIOLENCE IS EVERYONE'S PROBLEM AND THE SOLUTION IS UP TO EVERYONE.

In supporting the Fight Free mission, Donte Smith, from the Regional Community Relations Department of Church's Chicken, has contacted Dr. Peggy Dolan, President of Fight Free Schools, Inc., and offered to assist in supporting schools non-violent message. After collaborating with Dr. Dolan and through the approval of the Church's corporate office, the following outline is offered from Church's partnership:

• Church's will provide premiums (balloons, pencils, coloring books, etc.) for the participating school.

• Church's will provide the school with Merit Certificates for students who meet the Fight-Free requirements. (To be determined by the school principal.)

• Church's will provide the school with a KHFAAOOTY Bear.

• Church's will provide the school with a "Church's Supports Fight-Free Schools" banner.

• Church's will donate (*) proceeds from each meal sold on Fight-Free School Day(s) (Two separate days to be determined by the principal and coordinated by Church's representative.)

• Church's will provide the mascot "Churchie/Chica" at Fight-Free School assemblies.

• Church's will provide the "Chicken Bouncer" and "Churchie/Chica" for events surrounding Fight-Free Schools (assemblies, rallies, etc.) Subject to availability.

* Donations will go to the Fight-Free Schools Scholarship Fund in the name of Church's Chicken and the participating school.

We are also collaborating on a Write-Not-Fight form that will be included in the bags of chicken that are purchased at your school fund raiser. All fund raising donations for Fight-Free will go to a Fight-Free Scholarship Fund, sponsored by Church's Chicken. All Fight-Free students will be eligible. When available, applications for the Fight-Free Scholarship will be offered at area Church's Chicken locations. To be eligible, the student's principal must sign to verify that the applicant is indeed a Fight-Free student and a good citizen at school. We'll give you more details on the scholarships as they become available. In the meantime, if you are interested in involving your area Church's Chicken in a Fight-Free Partnership, please call Donte Smith at 618-257-2876. You will find working with Donte a pleasant experience, and the Board of Fight-Free Schools, Inc. salutes his efforts.

Fight Free Schools, Inc.
Board Member
Government Sponsor:
County Executive, Buzz Westfall

Fight Free Board of Directors
Dr. Peggy Dolan, President
Molly Bunton, Vice President
Ellen O'Sullivan, Treasurer
Mortimer J. Reilley, Director

Fight Free Front Staff
Peggy Dolan
Molly Bunton
Rosemary Teranova

LOCK IT UP!
For an effective and simple Fight-Free lesson, try this activity with your entire school:
"Attention all students at ____ School! You are invited to a lock up. In our school gym on (date), we are going to lock up all words and phrases that are not respectful. Each classroom is to brainstorm a list of "put down" words and negative sayings that do not reflect respect. Bring your list, and we will lock them up forever. We will replace them with words you brainstorm that show respect. We will fly respect words around our cafeteria walls. These might be words that KHFAAOOTY would say like: "I am sorry if I hurt your feelings.", "May I help you?", "Pardon me.", "Thank you.", "I appreciated your help."

This activity gets the kids talking and makes a great decoration for the

Lock It Up!

cafeteria as balloon shapes can be cut out of bright construction paper.

At the assembly, have the students notice that the "put down" phrases they use or hear are pretty much the same. Just as a smile is the same in any language, so, too, is a "put down." Let's talk respect. An activity such as this helps get everyone on the same page and gives a frame of reference when students do experience a conflict. "Now didn't we put this word in our lock-up box?" Dramatically lock the words up, and throw away the key. Teachers can discuss how "put down" words make people feel and how respectful words make people feel.

R
E
S
P
E
C
T

For lessons that go hand-in-hand with the Fight-Free message, check your PREP Character Education materials in the counseling office, available through the Cooperating School Districts.

"How to PREP" - Using Character Education in Schools, Homes, and Communities
Cooperating School Districts
13157 Olive Spur Road
St. Louis, MO 63141

STOP HANDGUN VIOLENCE

If you were told that trigger locks could save a child, wouldn't you run out and buy out the store? Freida Bernestein, founder of Missourians Against Handgun Violence, continues to herald the message of the need for trigger locks in Missouri. After the recent gun accidents in our area involving children, Frieda was seen on the Channel 5 morning show. Here is her message:

1. Always unload firearms carefully and completely <u>before</u> taking them into the home. Never load a firearm in your home.

- *Every two hours, someone's child is killed with a gun.*

2. Always make absolutely sure that firearms in your home are securely stored in a location inaccessible to children. Ammunition should be stored in a separate, locked location.

- *Every year, about 1,500 people are accidentally killed with guns.*

3. Always place firearms in their proper storage location immediately after returning from a hunting trip or a day at the range.

- *About 1.2 million elementary-aged latchkey children have access to guns when they come home from school.*

4. Always re-check firearms carefully and completely to confirm that they are still unloaded when you remove them from storage. Accidents have occurred when a family member has borrowed or loaned a firearm and returned it to storage while it was still loaded.

- *There are an estimated 200 million firearms in the possession of private citizens in the United States.*

5. Always remember: it is your responsibility to make certain the firearms in your home are not casually accessible to anyone, especially curious young people.

- *If you have a firearm in your home, protecting it from misuse is your responsibility.*

Your most important responsibility is ensuring that children cannot encounter loaded firearms. The precautions you take must be completely effective. Anything less invites tragedy.

Firearms kept for home security:
If you feel the need to keep a firearm available for home security, you should take special safety measures. Keeping a gun to defend your family doesn't make sense, if that same gun puts your family members or visitors at risk. Most fatal home firearm accidents occur when youngsters - often children who do not live in the home - discover firearms thought to be safely hidden or inaccessible.

Trigger locks are one effective, low-cost method of securing your firearms.

In addition to offering protection from tampering, trigger locks also:

- *prevent accidental discharge when a firearm is being loaded or cleaned*

- *make your firearms unattractive to*

Stop Handgun Violence

theft by making them inoperable.

"The time is right to stop handgun violence. Getting guns off he streets and away from our children is essential to reducing crime and saving lives and that requires eveyone's cooperative effort. Law enforcement officials want and need your help."

*—Clarence Harmon, President
Missourians Against Handgun
Violence*

<u>The Sad and Startling Statistics:</u>

• Of the approximately 1,000 firearm deaths in 1994 in Missouri, 164 involved children and young adult victims, including 17 youth under the age of 15. Of these deaths, 29 were accidental shootings.

• Every day in America, 14 children aged 19 and under are killed with firearms (almost 6,000 a year).

• The above statistics include only those killed—many more were injured (hospital emergency departments treat four children for gunshot wounds for every one child killed by gunfire.

• The rate of firearm deaths for children aged 14 and under is nearly 12 times higher in the U. S. than in 25 other industrialized countries combined.

• An estimated 1.2 million "latchkey"children (come home from school to a house without an adult) have access to unload and unlocked firearms.

• Twenty-five percent of 3-4 year olds, seventy percent of 5-6 year olds, and ninety percent of 7-8 year olds have been found to be strong enough to pull the trigger of some common handguns.

• The total cost of firearm-related deaths and injuries among children aged 14 and under is approximately $7 billion.

• One-half of unintentional shootings take place in the home of the victim—and 38% take place in the home of a friend or relative. It is not enough for a parent to store guns responsibly—the parents of friends must also!

• 91% of handguns involved in unintentional shootings come from the home where the shootings occur.

• Trigger locks are not effective in preventing unintentional shootings, they can also reduce juvenile suicide and homicide by helping to keep loaded, unlocked guns out of the hands of children.

The Missourians Against Handgun Violence believe that guns are too easy to obtain and too easy to use.

Seen in the Hallway of a school:
We are Drug Free,
We are Fight Free,
We are Gun Free.

<u>PEVELY STUDENTS KEEP FLAG FLYING HIGH</u>

This school year Pevely Primary students will face a new challenge: to use their heads, not their hands, to resolve conflicts. Pevely Primary officially began its quest to be a Fight-Free school on Monday, September 8, 1997. Implemented in schools throughout the nation, the program is designed to use positive reinforcement to discourage fighting among students. It was started by Peggy Dolan, a principal in the Hazelwood School District.

In individual classrooms, Principal Jeff Williams and Counselor Lesa Cruzado, introduced the program to the students and unveiled the flag that will fly outside the building signifying that Pevely Primary is a "Fight -Free School."

The teachers also post smaller flags on their classroom doors to indicate a Fight-Free classroom. If two or more students are involved in a fight they will take down the classroom flags and also accompany the prinicpal to take down the school flag. The next day, they will put the flags back up, symbolizing a new day as a Fight-Free school.

Throughout the school year, assemblies will be held at which students will receive incentives, prizes, certificates, etc., for remaining Fight-Free. School goals are also set and a school Fight-Free song is sung. The school counselor will also be implementing conflict resolution series into classroom guidance lessons, and daily the students and faculty are made aware of the number of Fight-Free students from the previous day.

Faculty members and students alike are responsible for the success of the program. Pevely Primary believes in the importance of giving students skills for managing and resolving conflict in the early grades. We hope the parents and community will join us in our effort to provide students with a safe, fight-free learning environment.

UPCOMING EVENTS
MAESP Conference
March 15 - 17, 1998
Tan-Tar-A
Osage Beach, MO

MCSA Sponsors
Fight Free Seminar
April 30, 1998
Rolla, MO
For information call Larch Farrill
(573) 556-6272

Illinois D.A.R.E. Officers
Conference
July 1998 - Peoria, IL

Fight-Free Baseball Games Coming Up!

TAKE US OUT TO THE BALLGAME!

tune: "Take Me Out to the Ballgame"

Take Me Out to the Ballgame

Take us out to the ballgame.
Fight-Free kids in the crowd.
We sure are hoping the Cardinals win,
We sure hope they won't have a fight again.
So let's keep the Fight-Free flag flying,
Thanks, Marty, for our tickets...and it's go, go, go Cardinals.
Go at the Fight-Free games!

The voucher system will be used as last year.
Details will be forwarded to you in the near future.

Night Games:

April 14 - Arizona Diamond Backs

April 28 - Montreal Expos

May 27 - Colorado Rockies

LET US KNOW
What Fight-Free information do you have to share with other Fight-free schools? Do you have a song, a jingle or a rap, an idea, an assembly, an incentive, a tip, a change, or a result? We learn from each other. Every conference or seminar that I present Fight-Free, I find out something new and different that works for their school. Please send us your Fight-Free news to include in future newsletters.

Send your information to:
Dr. Peggy Dolan
McNair Elementary School
585 Coachway Lane
Hazelwood, MO 63042
314-953-4700

Fight-Free Manual

School Violence...Calming the Storm, by Dr. Peggy Dolan will be available this spring.

For information, call Rising Sun Publications: 1-800-524-2813.

Fight-Free Thanks to:
Alvernys Watson, Asst. Principal at Keevan Elementary School

Rick Kreitner, Grannemann Elementary School Prinicpal
For serving as Fight-Free Seminar Presenters